Healing Ministry

A Practical Guide

To Anneke,
with blessings,
Jan Alkire

Healing Ministry
A Practical Guide

Leo Thomas, O.P.
with Jan Alkire

Sheed & Ward

Sheed & Ward™ is a service of The National Catholic Reporter Publishing Company.

◆

Library of Congress Cataloguing-in-Publication Data

Thomas, Leo, 1922-
    Healing ministry : a practical guide / Leo Thomas, with Jan Alkire.
        p.   cm.
    Rev. of : The healing team. c1987
    Includes bibliographical references.
    ISBN: 1-55612-673-5 (pbk. : alk. paper)
    1. Spiritual healing. 2. Church work with the sick.
3. Pentecostalism—Catholic Church.   I. Alkire, Jan. II. Thomas.
Leo, 1922- Healing team. III. Title.
BT732.5.T46 1994
259'.4—dc20   94-8763
                                                                    CIP

◆

Published by: Sheed & Ward
                 115 E. Armour Blvd.
                 P.O. Box 419492
                 Kansas City, MO 64141

To order, call: (800) 333-7373

Contents

Part II:
Spiritual Resources for Ministers of Religious Healing

Preface

❖　　❖　　❖　　❖　　❖

This book grows out of my experience of nearly thirty years of training both clergy and laity—Catholic and Protestant—to do pastoral ministry, and of my own priestly ministry to the needs of hurting Christians. Since 1977 I have been on the staff of The Institute for Christian Ministries, based in Tacoma, Washington, which offers a two-year training program entitled "Formation for Healing Ministry." Much of what I say in this book comes from this program; some comes from my own experience as practitioner and trainer in the ministry of religious healing.

Much has happened since *The Healing Team* was published in 1987. My goal back then was to place the ministry of religious healing squarely at the heart of the Church's ordinary ministry of pastoral care. That is now emerging. What once was a ministry that only charismatic Christians valued and practiced has begun to move into ordinary parish life. Non-charismatics are starting to hear a commission which Jesus gave his disciples 2,000 years ago, but which then fell on deaf ears for centuries. Today, thousands of lay and ordained people seek ways to bring the healing power of Christ back to where people go to encounter God— their parishes.

Also since 1987, another book of mine has been published, *Healing as a Parish Ministry* (Ave Maria Press, 1992). I co-authored it with writer Jan Alkire, with whom I have written the present work, *Healing Ministry*. Together, Jan and I modified the original version of *The Healing Team* in response to feedback from readers of both books. New features:

- At the suggestion of readers and prayer group leaders, we added reflection questions to each chapter. Individuals can use them to integrate healing into their lives and to deepen their spirituality. Prayer groups can use them as a study guide for teaching people how to engage in healing ministry.

- For those who want to delve deeper into the topics presented in this book, each chapter includes a list of suggested books that expand upon the subject covered in that chapter.

- In response to positive feedback about our chapter summaries in *Healing as a Parish Ministry*, we added summaries to this book as well. These can be used for a quick review of the book's contents, especially its practical how-to sections.

- In an effort to help Christians make full use of their God-given gifts, we added a chapter to this edition. Called "Spiritual Gifts," it explains the need for, and appropriate use of, *all* God's gifts—natural ones, virtues and charisms. A secondary goal in "Spiritual Gifts" is to bridge the gap that sometimes exists between charismatics and non-charismatics, so that they can engage in healing ministry together.

- Jan revised the original text to increase its readability.

- Finally, since *The Healing Team* first was published in 1987, experience has added to my knowledge about the subject of religious healing. This revised edition reflects my growth. But more than ever I am convinced about the basic thesis of the 1st edition, namely that the ministry of religious healing does not belong in the category of healing—it does not offer an alternative to the biomedical model of health care. Instead, this ministry belongs in the category of worship: its goal is to bring hurting people into an experience of God meeting them in their need.

*   *   *   *

Healing Ministry should prove useful to clergy and laity who are interested in learning how to make healing ministry a part of the Church's overall ministry of pastoral care. This would include:

- pastoral visitors to the sick
- parishioners who engage in grief ministry
- Eucharistic ministers who bring communion to homebound parishioners
- teams who pray with hurting parishioners
- prayer communities that want to develop a sound ministry of religious healing.

*   *   *   *

Throughout this book the word "minister" refers to any ministering person without reference to ordination. "Supplicant" indicates the recipient of ministry. For the sake of inclusive language, male and female pronouns alternate with each other in a generic way for both the minister and the supplicant.

Jan and I struggled with the fact that in the English language, any pronoun for God falls short of reality. Yet prose suffers severely if all pronouns are avoided. In the end we decided that, when necessary, we would use traditional pronouns for God.

Considerable care has been taken to disguise the cases described in these pages. If you think you recognize yourself or another in one of this book's stories, it is only because of the commonality of human experiences that we all share.

Leo Thomas, O.P.

Dedication

I dedicate this book to those who have helped me grow in knowledge and understanding of the ministry of religious healing, specifically:

- to Francis MacNutt and Agnes Sanford, pioneers in this field;
- to the late Thomas Klink, Chaplain of the Menninger Foundation Hospital, who taught me about compassionate pastoral care;
- to Christy and John Wolfe and Sheila Fabricant Linn, who helped me give birth to what eventually became the Institute for Christian Ministries; and
- to fellow staff members of the Institute for Christian Ministries in Tacoma, Washington: Dave and Iris Beardemphl, Jim Webster and the many associates who make ICM's programs possible.

ICM continues to shape my thinking.

Part I

The Ministry
of Religious Healing

1

Religious Healing vs. Faith Healing

❖   ❖   ❖   ❖   ❖

"Are you a psychic healer?"

"No."

"Are you a faith healer?"

"No, I'm not that either."

"What kind of healer are you?"

"Actually, I'm not a healer at all."

The audience to whom I was speaking looked surprised, but no one was more surprised by that last statement than I. I was getting ready to show a video tape of a team praying for a mother and her child who had had a traumatic birth. Before showing the video, I felt I needed to explain my ministry in the field of healing.

As a Roman Catholic priest, I often had anointed people with the "Last Sacrament." Prior to 1965, it was a ministry reserved for the dying. Recipients often panicked when I arrived with my oil and prayer book; they knew they must be dying or a priest wouldn't be there.

Then the church changed this official ministry to the sick and gave it a new name, *The Rite of Anointing and Pastoral Care of the Sick*. In the revised sacrament, priests anoint the sick and specifically pray for them to recover. What interested me about the new rite was the number of seriously ill people who, after receiving this sacrament, recovered dramatically.

About that same time, many Catholic and non-Catholic Christians became interested and successful in praying for healing. Their ministry was being shaped by numerous books on religious healing, the teaching of nationally recognized teachers on the subject and by various programs of training for healing ministry. Examples of their ministry to the sick were many and diverse:

- In a sports arena packed to the rafters a front row displayed a long line of wheel chairs. On the dais a woman in a flowing gown pronounced this one and that one and this one healed of arthritis, ruptured discs or tumors.
- In a cluttered living room a man, bald from chemotherapy, lay on a sofa while four friends knelt around him, read to him from the Bible, anointed him with oil and prayed for his healing.
- In a large parish church a priest called for everyone in the congregation who needed healing to come forward for the Sacrament of Anointing of the Sick. ·
- In a downtown hospital a woman received Holy Communion from a lay minister. They held hands and prayed for the woman's healing.
- In prayer groups around the country, hurting people would sit on a chair in the middle of the room while enthusiastic prayer group members gathered around them to pray (sometimes with great vigor) for healing to take place.

The above examples of the renewed practice of ministry to the sick sparked passionate reactions—favorable and unfavorable:

- Godfrey Diekmann, the editor of *Worship*, a sober, scholarly journal devoted to Christian worship, stated that one of his reasons for boundless optimism in the face of seeming cosmic disaster was the current manifestation of the power of the Holy Spirit which he could see in the renewed ministry of healing in the church.[1]

---

1. Diekmann, Geofrey, "The Laying on of Hands in Healing," *Liturgy: The Sick and the Dying*, 25:2 (March/April 1980): 7ff.

- In *A Doctor in Search of a Miracle*, William Nolen said that in following the career of Katherine Kuhlman for several years, he had not seen a single *miraculous* cure (emphasis added).[2]

- In his book, *Faith Healing*, Louis Rose stated, "After nearly twenty years of work I have yet to find one 'miracle cure'; and without that . . . I cannot be convinced of the efficacy of what is commonly termed faith healing."[3]

- In *The Power to Heal*, Francis MacNutt wrote that as a result of his ministry about 25% of the people prayed for indicate they are completely healed physically; about 50% say they are improved; while for about 25% no physical healing seems to happen.[4]

- Dennis and Matthew Linn, S.J. in collaboration with Barbara Shlemon, R.N. wrote a book titled *To Heal as Jesus Healed*[5] *whose main thrust is the power of the Sacrament of Anointing to effect physical as well as emotional and spiritual healing.*

- In *Prophetic Anointing*, James L. Empereur, S.J. said: "One can only wonder in what sense physical healing is really an *effect* of this sacrament (Anointing of the Sick). . . . This sacrament should not be surrounded with the kind of implicit hope or expectation that something miraculous might happen, even if it is only a happy side effect."[6]

Statements such as these revealed to me the wide variety of opinions in the Christian community regarding the ministry of religious healing. Behind this diversity lay a lack of agreement about the nature of this ministry. Also, I found that many differing theologies lay behind this ministry; no one had taken the time to examine them. So I began to study the question of what religious healing is.

---

2. Nolen, William, *Healing: A Doctor in Search of a Miracle*, New York, Random House, 1974.

3. Rose, Louis, *Faith Healing*, Penguin Books, 1971.

4. MacNutt, Francis, *Healing*, Notre Dame, Ave Maria Press, 1974, p. 28.

5. Shlemon, B.L., Linn, Dennis and Matthew, To Heal as Jesus Healed, Notre Dame, Ave Maria Press, 1978.

6. Empereur, James L., *Prophetic Anointing*, Wilmington, Michael Glazier Inc. 1982.

What Is Religious Healing?

When doing library research on this topic, I looked in the card catalogue under the subject heading of *healing*. Under this large heading, I saw subheadings such as *medical healing, surgical healing, psychic healing* and *religious or faith healing*. I accepted this way of listing religious healing for a long time, and in writing about it found that I thought of my ministry as just one more form of healing. That thinking lasted until I was in front of a group of health care workers which included physicians, psychologists and social workers, the group to whom I was speaking at the beginning of this chapter. Suddenly, I found myself declining to accept the title not only of *psychic healer* and *faith healer*, but of *healer* itself.

Instead, I made a startling discovery about religious healing, one that has changed my thinking, even my life. **The ministry of religious healing does not belong in the category of healing at all. It belongs in the *category of worship*.**

I was not a health care worker. My task as a minister of religious healing differed entirely from the medical people to whom I was speaking. I was not one of them. And I did not strive to offer an alternative to their system of health care as do, for example, Christian Scientists. When pressed to explain what I was if I was not a healer, I surprised myself again when, after a moment's reflection, I said, "I am a leader of worship." And that, I firmly believe, is what the minister of religious healing is.

What Happens in Worship

Randy, an engineer with the Boeing Company, came to the sacristy after Mass one Sunday and said something had happened to him during Mass. As I changed out of my vestments, he told me about his 20-year-old daughter. For a long time he had been feeling "kind of sick" about Rosie. Whenever he thought about her, he would get a tight feeling in the pit of his stomach. She wouldn't go to college, wouldn't get anything more than a part-time waitress job, socialized with rude, undesirable friends, and wouldn't listen to anything Randy said to her.

"But today as I was kneeling there not even thinking about my daughter," said Randy, "I actually heard God speaking to me. He said, 'I want you to trust me with Rosie's life.' And I knew it was God who'd spoken to me and that I could trust Him to help Rosie. Right then and there the tight feeling in the pit of my stomach went away."[7]

What happened to Randy *should* happen in worship. He experienced God's presence and it brought healing. **The purpose of worship is to enable a person—or a whole community of persons—to come before God with a need and to experience God meeting that need in the most loving way possible.**

For example, in Sunday worship a community comes before the Lord with a need to feed upon the Bread of Life. By the use of sacred space—a special building; by the use of music, singing, color, candles; by the proclamation of God's word; by sharing at the Lord's table, we experience God meeting our need. We are fed; we are strengthened. We go forth with new-found strength to continue walking as disciples of Christ. Baptisms, weddings and funerals are examples of official worship designed to meet specific needs.

Suffering Christians

Through my research and the ensuing years of practice, it became clear to me that the ministry of religious healing is meant to enable the person who is hurting—physically, emotionally, spiritually—to experience the Lord meeting her in her need. If the minister uses the many resources at his disposal well, the supplicant (i.e. the person receiving the ministry of prayer for healing) experiences God meeting her in her need.

- She will first of all experience God loving and caring for her.
- Her sense of hopelessness and helplessness will be overcome and she will experience the renewed power of hope.

---

7. "Hearing" God's voice is a form of praying with imagery, which I discuss in Chapter 2.

- She will experience the presence of Jesus in the fellowship of believers ministering to her; of believers loving her, valuing her.
- Each one of these effects of worship will affect her powerfully in her total person and healing is to be expected.

The truth that this ministry belongs in the category of worship rather than in healing has many practical consequences. The main one is that it gives us clarity about who we are and what we are doing. It makes a great difference whether we think of ourselves as health care workers making therapeutic interventions or whether we understand ourselves to be ministers who are enabling a suffering Christian to experience God meeting her in her need.

The health care worker measures the success of therapy by the degree of improvement of the patient's ailment. The minister of religious healing measures the success of his ministry not by the degree of improvement of the ailment, but by the extent to which the supplicant experiences God meeting her in her need.

Some time ago a newspaper article told of a child who died because after his parents prayed for him, they withdrew his medicine, believing that prayer had healed him. Mistaken thinking like this about the ministry of religious healing, if left uncorrected, will destroy it. The boy's parents thought of themselves as offering an alternative to medical treatment.

We who minister religious healing are *not* offering an alternative form of treatment; we are not practicing medicine without a license. However, a supplicant *should* expect healing. Likewise, a doctor should expect that if he does his work well the patient will experience being cared for by God. While both bring healing, the minister and the doctor are doing different things.

A Vulnerable Ministry

Godfrey Diekmann (quoted earlier in this chapter) is right. The power of the Holy Spirit *is* being manifested in the ministry of healing in the church. People are encountering the trans-forming power of Jesus in ways never expected just a few years ago. But the ministry of religious healing is a newborn infant, tender and vulnerable. We must learn what we are doing or we can kill it. Both William Nolen and Louis Rose (quoted earlier) illustrate this destructive misunderstanding of this ministry by their preoccupation with miracles. Their misunderstanding is common both within and outside of religious circles. They lead people to believe that the ministry of religious healing is about "miracles."

For example, a woman brought her 13-year-old daughter, Tina, to us for prayer ministry. For several months since a fall from a horse, Tina had been unable to use her left arm. We were dismayed to discover that the mother had never taken Tina to a doctor. She said, "I just know God's going to heal my daughter through prayer."

At our insistence, the mother sought a doctor's help. A simple surgical procedure followed by intensive therapy brought near-normal movement back into Tina's arm. We prayed for Tina throughout this process and helped her overcome the re-sentment of God she had developed during the time she had remained unhealed.

"Looking for miracles" means focusing upon an event so sensational that it forces faith from the observer. This fascina-tion with the sensational distressed and sometimes angered Jesus: "How evil are the people of this day! They ask for a miracle, but none will be given them except the miracle of Jonah." (TEV, Lk 11:29)

This book is not about "miracles." The ministry of religious healing described in this book is not about performing miracles. The ministry this book advocates must be seen in the context of overall pastoral care. When Jesus rehabilitated and commis-sioned the repentant Simon-Peter after the Resurrection, he did not say, "Work miracles." Rather, he said, "Tend my sheep."(NAB, Jn 21:16) And when Jesus described himself, he did not say, "I am a miracle worker." Instead, he said, "I have come in order that you might have life—life in all its fullness. . . . I am the good shepherd. As the Father knows me and I know the Father, in the same way I know my sheep and they know me. And I am willing to die for them." (TEV, Jn 10:10b, 14-15)

Real healing occurs in pastoral healing ministry, but it can be measured only in the context of the way the Good Shepherd cares for his sheep, not in the context of what a good physician does for his patient. That is why the ministry of religious healing is not a substitute for medical treatment but is often a hand-in-hand partner with medicine.

Pastoral healing ministry, offered with sensitivity and competence, does produce results. I've seen the healing power of Jesus dramatically transforming people's lives. This transformation manifests itself physically, emotionally, spiritually and in relationships. The recipients of the ministry, and those close to them, recognize God's power at work. They experience the care of a loving Father: they know they have been loved and cared for. They see themselves being healed in ways they had never expected.

God Is With Us: God Uses Us

If the ministry of religious healing is to bear the fruit that God intends, a correct understanding of the Incarnation is essential. **The Incarnation is the model for all of our Christian activity in this world.** By the Incarnation I mean all that is implied in the text: "The Word became a human being and . . . lived among us." (TEV, Jn 1:14) Everything changed radically when God took on a human nature, became a human baby, grew into a child, a teenager, a young adult. His humanness has given us a new way of thinking and acting. God chose to reveal himself through created things. Rather than being a one-time event, this is the model God uses for all further activity in the world.

The Incarnation is the basis of our use of sacraments and sacramentals. The abundant life which Christ came to bring, now that He is risen and at the right hand of the Father, continues through the church's use of water, bread and wine, oil, touch, music—in fact, through every created being.

This truth has profound implications for our ministry. I call this an incarnational, God-with-us attitude. Without an incarnational attitude, we are reduced to merely interceding for some-one to God. Some ministers, in fact, see intercession as the only action on the part of human ministers who are praying for heal-ing. They see themselves in this way:

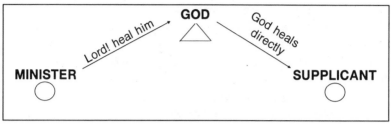

Figure 1[8]

The incarnational attitude, however, sees that God uses us to achieve His work. Petition is only one of the ways that we minister healing. God works *through* us in such a way that an action comes totally from God and totally from us. So the slogan "only God heals" is false. The following diagram illustrates the incarnational approach to religious healing:

Figure 2

Jesus demonstrated this point when he said, "As the Father sent me, so I send you."(TEV, Jn 20:21b) Then he breathed on them and said, "Receive the Holy Spirit." We are the fullness of Christ, i.e., the Body of Christ. We are the members, He the head. The task the Father gave His Son continues in the com-mission Christ has given us: "Jesus called his twelve disciples to-

---

8. This diagram appears in Chapter 8 of Francis MacNutt's *Healing* (Ave Maria Press, 1974).

gether and gave them authority to . . . heal every disease and every sickness."(TEV, Mt 10:1) By the power of the Holy Spirit, God remains in the world through His church. We who have received the message of Christ in faith are that church.

We have not begun to realize the dignity that is ours, a dignity that carries a very remarkable responsibility. Our eyes are the eyes that God uses to weep for the pain of the world. Our emotions are the emotions God uses to have compassion upon his people. Our hands are the hands God uses to bestow his healing blessing upon those in need.[9]

If we do not weep, some people will never know God cares. If we do not lay our hands on others in a gesture of acceptance, some will never experience healing in this world. We have the ability to let God use us to build up his kingdom; we also have the freedom to refuse, and thus hinder the coming of God's kingdom. This is the mystery of the Incarnation: God will establish his presence in the world through the weakness and the limitations of sinful humanity.

My friend Barbara wrote down how Jesus' love became real to her through the compassion of a neighbor:

> When I was in my late forties, my husband died suddenly. For the next two or three weeks a lot of people came and went from my house—relatives, my priest, friends and neighbors, a business consultant. Many things had to be taken care of. Then everything was quiet. The one daughter still living at home was in school all day. I wandered around the house feeling numb and lost. I prayed and went to church a lot but couldn't get my bearings.
>
> Many times I walked a few blocks to my friend Christy's house. She was young with three small children, and I usually found her busy with housework. She would stop and we would go into her living room to chat. I would sit in a rocking chair and she would sit on a big footstool in front of me. Some days I couldn't talk. I

---

9. For an excellent biblical explanation of the Body of Christ, see William Barclay's *The Mind of St. Paul* (San Francisco, Harper, 1958, pp. 241-251).

would just sit with my head in my hands. She would put her arms around me and hold me. Sometimes she would rock us gently and say things like: 'Jesus, help Barbara feel your deep love for her; to know your heart grieves with her heart; to know you are here.' I only stayed about twenty minutes or so.

One day as I was walking back home I stopped dead still. It suddenly hit me: that was Jesus! He was using Christy's arms to love and comfort me. No wonder he seemed so close and so real. He was. In her!

God *is* with us all. In my journey in this area of healing, God has taken me on a route I'd never considered years ago. He's shown me that healing happens in the context of worship. When ministered with compassion, it brings relational, spiritual, emotional and physical health. Ministers of religious healing are those people of God who reach out and touch the lives of the hurting people in their world.[10]

For Further Reading

1. *The Prayer that Heals,* by Francis Macnutt. Ave Maria Press, 1981.

2. *Healing Prayer,* by Barbara Leahy Shlemon. Ave Maria Press, 1976.

---

10. Chapters 2, 5 and 6 of *Healing as a Parish Ministry* (Thomas and Alkire, Ave Maria Press, Notre Dame, 1992) go into greater detail about the incarnational model of ministry, the power of community, and the fact that the ministry of religious healing belongs in the category of worship.

Summary—Chapter 1

A. This chapter asserts that the ministry of religious healing belongs in the category of worship.

   1. The purpose of worship is to enable a person—or a whole community of persons—to come before God with a need and to experience God meeting that need in the most loving way possible.

   2. The ministry of religious healing is meant to enable the person who is hurting—physically, emotionally or spiritually—to experience the Lord meeting her in her need. Therefore, success in healing ministry must be measured not by the degree of improvement of an ailment, but by the extent to which the supplicant experiences God meeting her in her need.

   3. Religious healing is not a ministry that stands alone. It needs to be practiced in the context of overall pastoral care.

B. The Incarnation is the model for the ministry of religious healing.

   1. A *non*-incarnational model sees intercession as the only action by human ministers praying for healing.

   2. An incarnational model sees that God makes use of us to achieve his work. God works through us in such a way that the action is totally God's and totally ours. We are the Body of Christ, with Christ as our head. The task that the Father gave to his Son continues in and through us today.

For Your Reflection—Chapter 1

1. Recall a time when you, a friend or a loved one was ill. Did religion play any part in the healing of this illness? What was most helpful? What was least helpful? What other healing ministry does this chapter suggest that would have been helpful?

2. For an example of religious healing, read Luke 17:11-19. Imagine yourself being one of the ten lepers or a bystander. How do you experience God in this scene? In your role as a leper or a bystander, how (if at all) is this an experience of worship for you?

3. This chapter says, "If we do not weep, some people will never know God cares. If we do not lay our hands on others in a gesture of acceptance, some will never experience healing in this world." Do you agree or disagree with this statement? Why?

2

How to Minister as a Team[1]

❖   ❖   ❖   ❖   ❖

Gloria had been a serious dance student since the age of five.
To make room in her life for lessons and for 30 hours of practice
per week, she had made many sacrifices: few leisurely girlhood
chats, no free time after school, no pastimes such as skiing or
skating. As Gloria grew up, the only thing more important to
her than dancing was her deep relationship with the Lord.

Prayer, hard work and talent held hands so successfully that
by the age of twenty, Gloria was dancing professionally on the
New York stage. Then during a dress rehearsal the one thing
dancers most dread happened: a knee injury. She obeyed doctor's orders to stay off the stage so her knee could heal, but at
the end of six weeks the joint remained swollen and painful. Discouraged because her future as a dancer seemed lost, she returned to her parent's home, contacted our team, and asked us
to pray with her for healing. This chapter uses Gloria as an example of what to do in team ministry and how to do it.

---

1. Author's note: This chapter gives a detailed description of the process of
team ministry. In a number of places, I note the use of specific gifts of the Holy
Spirit. If you are unfamiliar with these gifts and their use in prayer ministry, I
suggest you read Chapter 18 prior to reading this one.

Team Ministry

One of the questions most frequently asked of us is "Why do you minister as a team?" I strongly encourage team ministry for the following reasons:

- Healing flows from the Body of Christ, and a team represents Christ's Body. Christ, the Head, uses two, three or four of His members to heal a wounded member of His Body. But the team is not just any two or three people grouped together for the occasion of this ministry. As part of the Body of Christ, it has a life of its own which is animated by the Holy Spirit. This life must be nourished by time spent together in prayer, in reflection upon its ministry, in working out relationships and, perhaps, in some social time together.

- As described in Chapter 1, when healing flows from the Body of Christ, prayer is more than intercession. It makes Jesus *present* to the supplicant. This incarnational (God-with-us) theology undergirds team ministry.

- A team is a more effective channel of Christ's healing power. The unique personality, talents, virtues and charisms of several people can make Jesus more real to the supplicant than can one person's gifts.

- Team members draw courage and support from one another. What they might hesitate to attempt alone, they are more willing to attempt in a team.

- Finally, functioning as a team helps protect the supplicant from the blindness and woundedness of any one individual. Other team members can counterbalance one member's flaws, can alert them when they are inflicting their woundedness on a supplicant.

How to Minister as a Team

After discovering the value of team ministry and its goal of making Jesus real to the supplicant, the next question most people have is, "How does a team do that?" No rigid formula guarantees success, but certain ingredients are commonly present in prayer for healing. Sometimes all are used, sometimes one, sometimes another. Using Gloria as an example, here are the key elements in team ministry. (NOTE: Although this chapter describes team ministry, in some situations it is not feasible to operate as a team. Clergy, counselors, eucharistic ministers and pastoral visitors to the sick can adapt much of what is said here to a solo ministry.)

1. Prepare the Team

A half hour before Gloria's arrival, our team (Jim, Dave, Iris and I) met to prepare for ministry. We had chosen a conference room where no phone could interrupt us and no one could over-hear our ministry. Our first task was to create a sacred space that would heighten Gloria's ability to experience God's love and care.

So we set a table with a bouquet of flowers, a crucifix, a flask of blessed oil, a cup of blessed water, a container of blessed salt and a lighted, blessed candle. A banner proclaimed "Jesus Is Lord." Jim put five chairs in a circle, and Dave arranged soft lighting for the room.

Next, we chose a leader—this time me—and decided on practical matters, such as how many sessions we could offer and when they would be. Getting this far had taken only a few minutes. We spent the rest of the half hour in prayer, preparing ourselves for ministry. With Jim playing his guitar and leading our singing, we praised God in song and in prayer for ten minutes.

Spontaneously we fell silent and I, as leader, encouraged all of us to listen to the Lord for any messages God might have for us. Iris said she could mentally see an image of a rainbow with God as Father. The Father was standing behind the rainbow smiling on His children. Dave said he could sense Jesus walking among us, reaching out and touching each of us with His right hand.[2]

---

2. "Seeing" a rainbow, "sensing" God's presence, and "hearing" God's voice are forms of imaginative prayer, sometimes called praying with imagery. I cover this prayer form later in this chapter and also in Chapter 6 of *Healing as a Parish Ministry*.

I asked Jim to lead us in a song of praise in thanksgiving for God's encouragement. Then Dave anointed us with blessed oil. He made the sign of the cross on each of our foreheads and prayed for special gifts for each of us in our ministry to Gloria.

Before ending team preparation, I asked if anyone felt burdened in a way that might interfere with the ministry. One person said yes. At once, another team member prayed, "Lord, please lift this burden. Let each of us be a clear channel of your healing love."

Discussion about team preparation: The preparatory phase is an often overlooked, yet vital ingredient in the ministry of religious healing. Usually preparation begins by creating a sacred space, because few prayer teams have a special area already set aside for ministry. Normally we meet in classrooms, church basements, sewing rooms—whatever is available and private. With a little effort, we can transform these ordinary places into holy ones. A readied room should also include useful objects, e.g. a box of tissues (supplicants sometimes weep) and a note pad and pen (for writing down a Scripture or an appointment time)

All of this is external preparation. God's presence makes the space sacred. Prayer forms such as song, praise, Scripture and anointing will bring the team into God's presence.

Either before or after prayer, practical matters need to be addressed, e.g., designating who will be the team leader and reviewing what is already known about the supplicant. Having completed the preparatory phase of ministry, the team is ready to meet the supplicant.

2. Welcome the supplicant

We welcomed Gloria into our circle, and she took a seat between Jim and Dave. We all knew her, so there was no need for introductions. Also, she had experienced prayer ministry before, so we did not need to give much explanation. I told her we would pray with her for about an hour.

After asking and receiving Gloria's permission to hold hands for a brief opening prayer, I prayed for God to gather us into one Body and let his Holy Spirit empower us to minister the healing presence of Jesus. I prayed that Gloria might be open to receive any gift that God wished to give her.

Discussion: The process of welcoming the supplicant varies, depending on how well he knows the team and how much he knows about prayer ministry. If the supplicant and team members are not acquainted, introductions need to be made. Names, family status, church affiliation, connections through mutual friends are shared. (The team members should be wearing name tags so the supplicant can learn the names quickly.) Introductions should be brief and take no more than several minutes. Small talk or chattiness will *not* put the supplicant at ease. It confuses the issue of why he is here. This, in turn, increases his anxiety.

If the supplicant has not experienced the ministry of religious healing, briefly describe what will happen in the session. For example,

- explain that there will be a short time of prayer at the beginning, a time when he can state his need, and then the team will pray for healing.
- Inform him how long the session will last.
- Let him know how he can participate in the prayer time. Some people are terrified to pray out loud and are relieved to know they don't have to.
- Invite the supplicant to ask clarifying questions.
- Ask him to report what he is experiencing as the team prays for him.
- Tell him what to do if he needs to stand up for a moment or wants to use the restroom.

The above details tend to reduce anxiety because they explain what to expect. They give the supplicant as much control of the situation as possible. The attitude of the team is one of offering hospitality to a weary and wounded traveler on a spiritual journey.

Before moving into the listening phase of ministry, it is good to come into the presence of the Lord for a minute or two and seek the guidance of the Holy Spirit. You may also pray that the supplicant may know the presence of Jesus during this time of ministry.

3. Listen

After welcoming Gloria into our midst and saying a short opening prayer, I asked her in what way she would like us to pray. We already knew she was there for her knee, but we wanted a bit more detail. In particular, we were seeking information about Gloria's response to her injury. Was she depressed? Was she angry with God because of the accident? Was she worried about this being the end of her career? Gloria told us she felt discouraged at first, but she wasn't feeling depressed and she did not blame God for the injury. This information helped us decide what to pray for.

Discussion: When moving into the listening phase of ministry, the leader of the prayer team usually asks the supplicant what he is seeking ministry for. The team's task at this point is to facilitate the person telling his story in a way that will, in itself, be healing. Help him tell his story so that he doesn't get caught in a long monologue of unimportant details, or feel alone as he talks while the team silently looks on. Some questions may be necessary for clarification or to help the person having difficulty in telling his story. But avoid asking too many questions or it will no longer be his story but merely a question-and-answer session.

Attentive listening frees the supplicant to express not only facts, but deep feelings which accompany the facts. As a result of listening, we should be able to say to him, in essence, "This is how it feels to be you," in such a way that the person can say, "Yes! You have understood." To be heard is the beginning of the healing process.

Careful listening will help us begin to answer these questions:

- Are we the ones to pray?
- Is this the right time to pray?
- What should we pray for?

Listening is not just a phase that's done once then left be-hind. Ministers of prayer must constantly listen, both to the sup-plicant *and* to God. There is so much to listen to. The suppli-cant frequently gives new information; he reports to the team his experience of God working in him as the team prays. The team, too, experiences God giving them guidance as to the direction the ministry should take. (Note: Chapters 4 and 5 discuss listen-ing in greater detail.)

4. Make an agreement about ministry

After listening to Gloria and becoming aware that her injury was not causing her significant emotional or spiritual pain, I said it seemed that her only need for prayer was for physical healing for her injured knee. Since her time was limited (she needed to return to New York), I proposed that for an hour each day for one week, our prayer team could meet with her in the confer-ence room to pray for physical healing for her knee. Both Gloria and the rest of the team concurred with my proposal.

Discussion: The supplicant plays a key role in an agreement about ministry because the ministry of religious healing is not something we do *to* a supplicant. Rather, he is actively involved in the process of deciding upon a plan of action. An agreement should include several items which will give shape to our time together. Ministry will be chaotic and disorderly and have little chance of being effective if we do not reach an agreement with a supplicant about the following points:

- Where the ministry takes place.
- Who offers the ministry (i.e. what team members).
- What hurt will be ministered to.
- When and how long ministry will occur. Ministers frequently fail to specify a time limit; the failure to do so allows even the best of ministry to fall into chaos. Both the team and the supplicant should know when they will meet, for how long, and for how many sessions. (Prayer for healing often requires more than one session—See Chapter 8).

Many people avoid setting a definite length of time for ministry, thinking that they will "just be led by the Spirit" or that it might seem unloving to specify times. However, known limits are quite comforting for both team and supplicant. All of us have other obligations and we must place our ministry in the context of them. Also, time limits allow both the supplicant and the team to pace themselves. A supplicant can become anxious if he does not know how long the prayer team will continue; he is not sure whether he is imposing on the others, and he does not know how much to expect from them.

A team is more effective when operating within definite time frames. The style of ministering differs greatly if it is to be done in five minutes or in one hour. When working with an adult, forty minutes to an hour is about the right amount of time. In the initial meeting, or even before the initial meeting, they need to convey to the supplicant that they are willing to meet three, perhaps four, times, after which the team and supplicant will evaluate whether or not more ministry is needed. At the end of the first session the root cause of the distress may not yet be known, but there should be some understanding of the direction the ministry is going.

When the need for prayer has been discerned, and a plan of action has been devised for ministering to that need, it is helpful for the leader to articulate his understanding of how to proceed. His understanding should be confirmed by the team and needs to be agreeable to the supplicant. We must make sure that the supplicant is in wholehearted agreement with our plan of action. *We should never pray for healing of something that the supplicant does not want prayer for.*

In reaching an agreement about ministry, some teams worry about losing sensitivity to the supplicant and sounding impersonal. In fact, an agreement about ministry is part of taking care of a supplicant. It's one of the ways we convey Jesus' presence and loving concern for him.

5. Become a worshipping community

Having made an agreement with Gloria, I invited everyone to come into God's presence and focus especially on the presence of Jesus. Jim led us into five or ten minutes of gentle praise in song and praise prayers. Since Gloria was not comfortable with a charismatic style of praying we did not use our prayer language aloud.[3]

Discussion: Coming into God's presence is a crucial part of ministry. As with any worshipping community, we can do this a number of ways, e.g., concentrate our thoughts upon the presence of Jesus, and praise God with music and song. If no one plays a musical instrument, recorded music and a tape recorder can be used. Music eases our anxieties, puts us in a meditative frame of mind, and makes it easier to concentrate upon God's presence. Singing is a way of joining together; we do something in unison. And because most of us are timid about singing, it is a way of "risking" something of ourselves with others.

6. Enter into the heart of worship/ministry

Once everyone seemed united in worship, I began a prayer of affirmation for Gloria. "Thank you, God, for Gloria's deep faith. Thank you for her trust in your power to heal." Dave and Iris, who had known Gloria for a long time, both thanked God for her love of Him, her gift of dance, her self-discipline, her kindness to others, and for her sweet spirit.

After about five minutes of affirmation prayer[4] we started to pray in specific and detailed ways for the healing of the injured knee. With Gloria's permission, we gathered closely around her, laid our hands on her, and held in mind the image of Jesus reaching out and touching her knee. Each of us prayed in different ways. Jim prayed for God to bring healing to this injured member of his Body. Iris prayed for Jesus to restore total healing to Gloria's wound.

---

3. By "prayer language" I mean the charism of the gift of tongues, sometimes called "glossolalia." This is one of the Gifts of the Holy Spirit which I discuss in Chapter 18.

4. Chapter 14 goes into detail about the prayer of affirmation.

We spoke directly to Gloria's body and encouraged it to stir up within itself all the healing powers that Jesus had placed there. I prayed, "Body, restore the tissue, cells grow and bring healing, blood bring nourishment to the injured area."[5]

Dave anointed Gloria's knee with blessed oil and we all placed our hands on her knee and prayed silently. I suggested we sit down and become quiet and see if the Lord had some message for Gloria. Jim strummed on his guitar but we didn't sing. After some minutes of quiet, I asked Gloria what she had been experiencing. She replied that she felt warmth in her knee when Dave anointed it and laid his hands on it. Also, she said she had a "wonderful conviction" that the Lord was healing her.

Dave read a passage from Scripture which he believed the Lord wanted Gloria to hear. It expressed how very much God loved her. Again Iris reported seeing an image of a rainbow. This time one end of the rainbow was actually touching Gloria's knee.

Discussion: When we enter into the heart of worship we discover a rich variety of prayer. Before praying for a supplicant's specific need, I always begin this part of ministry with *prayers of affirmation.* This reveals to the person the goodness that God has placed in him; he will begin to experience the love that God has for him. Love, in itself, is a healing force.

Prayers of affirmation touch more than the supplicant. As ministers pray this prayer, they find themselves standing in awe of what God has done in this person. They find their own expectancy increased. They grow in love and compassion for the supplicant.

The next step in praying for healing is the *prayer of intercession.* This should be specific and concrete. In Gloria's case, we prayed for the torn tissue to be restored, for cells to grow and the blood to bring nourishment to the injured area. The more ministers know about the workings of the human person—mind and body—the better they can pray in this fashion.

---

5. Speaking directly to a supplicant's body is called a "prayer of command." It is a form of praying with imagery that helps ministers and supplicant's "see" or "sense" a part of the supplicant's body being restored to health.

Imaginative prayer (also called *praying with imagery*) is a powerful resource in healing ministry. Incarnational theology tells us that Christ, our Head, uses us to heal a member of His Body. But we are not lifeless puppets being manipulated by a Divine Puppeteer. Rather, God uses us as we really are, fully human persons. When God created us in His image, He gave us minds and wills to be used creatively. To create, we must have the ability to imagine. An architect must be able to "see" what a house will look like before she can draw up its blueprints. The minister of religious healing must be able to "see" the healed condition of the supplicant before she can pray for it.

A minister focusing upon a hurt while praying is like an architect mourning the absence of houses for homeless people. Both will fail in their goal of meeting a need. Architects have to imagine the detailed processes by which houses will be built, how the contractor will put in foundations, how the carpenters will build with wood. In the same way, the minister of prayer needs to imagine Christ at work in the healing process. She may imagine Him touching or laying His hands on an injured part. She may imagine Jesus pouring light into the darkness of the supplicant's life, or activating the natural processes of the human body to destroy cancerous cells.

The team should also instruct the supplicant how to pray imaginatively, both during the time of ministry and in between times. When people are hurting, they frequently need support and encouragement to pray the prayer of faith rather than the prayer of desperation. In short, praying with imagery "prays the solution, not the problem."[6]

Touch contributes a great deal to the effectiveness of the ministry of religious healing. For 2,000 years the Church has used "laying on of hands" as an action that conveys God's presence and care. Jesus often laid his hands on the sick when he healed them. (cf. Mt 8:15; Mk 1:41; Lk 8:54)

Make sure the supplicant is comfortable with being touched before doing so! When you have his permission, lay your hands

---

6. Chapter 6 of *Healing as a Parish Ministry* (op. cit.) goes into greater detail about imaginative prayer.

lightly and lovingly on the head or shoulders. You communicate more of your self with touch than you do with words.

Sometimes the supplicant will experience warmth or a tingling sensation when touch is used. Sometimes the hands of the minister will tremble slightly. Many ministers and supplicants value these signs highly because they interpret them as signs of divine power at work. In my opinion, a gentle touch that conveys love and compassion is a surer sign of God's presence than trembling hands or tingling warmth.

The sense of God's presence may be enhanced if the minister prays imaginatively when touching the supplicant, e.g. "Jesus, as I lay my hands upon Your friend, may he know that You are reaching out to touch this hurt, to heal it. Use my hand to convey Your love for Your friend."[7]

Sacramentals, such as blessed candles, water, oil or salt, can make God's presence and power more real to a supplicant. Use them creatively and avoid an empty ritualistic use, devoid of meaning. People sometimes ask me how to use sacramentals, implying that there is *one* correct way, and if the team uses them in this way there will be some infallible results. This is a wrong way of thinking.

The first guiding principle governing the use of sacramentals is to use them in ways that will stir up hope in the supplicant and in the team. The second guiding principle is to administer them with so much love and compassion that the supplicant will more fully experience God's love for him.

A sacramental should be administered with a dignity, and even solemnity, that will enhance its symbolism. The effectiveness of religious symbols diminishes if we use them carelessly. For example, anointing with oil from a tiny vial carried in a pocket or purse reduces the impact of this symbol. In team ministry I advocate a prominent display of sacramentals in attractive containers.

Make sure the supplicant understands what sacramentals are and has a correct understanding of their use. You may need

---

7. Chapter 16 goes into greater detail about the appropriate use of touch in healing ministry.

to explain what they are and how to use them in faith. I remember one man who walked into our prayer room for his first ministry session. The room was dimly lit and a lighted candle was on the table. Looking shocked, he asked, "What is this, a seance?"

If a supplicant does not understand sacramentals, he can get quite upset when they are used with him in ministry. However, when explained and used with faith and love, most supplicants appreciate them and report great benefits from their use. Sometimes it's good to give the supplicant a sacramental—such as a bottle of oil or holy water or a blessed candle—to take home. Instruct him to use it daily with prayer for a continuation of the healing begun in this time of ministry.[8]

In ending this discussion on prayer forms commonly used in ministry, keep in mind that your ministry will not always follow the order given here. You might bless the supplicant with Holy Water at the very beginning of ministry. You may use song and music and the prayer of affirmation at various times throughout ministry. The prayers described here are not a formula to be followed rigidly. Rather, they are elements that must be constructed into a meaningful time of worship in which Christ is experienced meeting the needs of the supplicant.

7. Do closure

Towards the end of our scheduled time with Gloria, I sensed we'd done all we needed to do in this prayer time. I asked the team and Gloria if they felt we'd finished our ministry. Everyone agreed. I suggested we give thanks to God for what He had done during our hour together. Together we sang a song of thanks.

Before Gloria left, I asked her if something had been especially helpful that night. She said the anointing with oil had seemed the most helpful. Then I asked her if anything had been *un*helpful. She shook her head.

We made an agreement with her about the next time we'd meet for prayer and how many sessions would follow. I stood up

---

8. Chapter 15 goes into greater detail about the use of sacramentals in healing ministry.

to indicate the time of ministry was over, then each of us hugged her and said good-bye.

Discussion: As ministry comes to an end, certain things should be done. Ask the supplicant what has been especially helpful to him in this ministry, and what has been unhelpful. These questions help him reflect on what God has done, when and where God has been most present. It gives the team feedback it needs to evaluate the effectiveness of its ministry. It also gives clues as to how to minister to this supplicant in the future. Asking what had been unhelpful gives the supplicant a chance to give the team negative feedback that he otherwise would be unwilling to give.

Practical arrangements about any future ministry should be reviewed with the supplicant. Then spend a short time giving thanks to God for the healing process He has begun.

Farewells and leave-taking are important, but should not be drawn out. The team leader will have to take charge, since most supplicants find it hard to disengage from ministry and will want to socialize. The easiest way to disengage is to be straightforward with the supplicant. Say something like, "We need to listen to the Lord about our ministry and to give thanks to Him before we leave, so we need to say good-bye to you now." If the team stands and embraces, or shakes hands, with the supplicant, it is easier for him to leave.

8. Debrief

After Gloria left, our team remained for a time of debriefing. I started by asking how everyone thought it went. Jim and Dave and Iris all agreed it had been a good time of ministry. Then I asked if there was something that anyone would have liked to have done differently. Dave thought we could have made more use of the Scripture text by helping Gloria understand more fully what God was saying to her.

After talking about this, I asked the team to reflect on those places where God was most evident and where the gifts were especially noticeable. I began by affirming Dave for his gentle yet powerful anointing of Gloria. I told Iris I had sensed deep compassion in her prayers of intercession. To Jim I said that the songs he used were appropriate and helpful in furthering the time of prayer.

The others reviewed how the Lord had guided us in team prayer. We talked briefly about future meetings with Gloria, sensing that frequent and prolonged prayer was necessary to complete this healing. We gave thanks to God for all he had done and brought our meeting to an end.

Discussion: After the supplicant leaves, the team needs to debrief. The team leader will help the team review how they functioned as a team. She will affirm each member's ministry and point out instances of God working through each member. She will encourage the team to do this for one another by mentioning some specific gift of ministry, such as a vision, a prayer, or an act of compassion. The emphasis should be on affirmation, not on shortcomings and deficiencies. If there is any future ministry with this supplicant, discuss what direction the ministry should take.

During debriefing, the leader should inquire if any team member is burdened as a result of ministry. If so, the team should pray that he be released. End the session by saying a short prayer of thanks for continued growth for themselves as a team and pray for any needed gifts.

Results of ministry to Gloria: Altogether, we met with Gloria six times. Her healing was gradual, but complete. She returned to dancing with no further problem.

Conclusion

As you read all of the ingredients needed for effective team ministry, you may feel overwhelmed. You may ask yourself how you can ever master all of this. The process really is not that complicated. I did not invent the various ingredients. Rather, I identified and named the items that come naturally as a team prays. Identifying and naming what is natural creates a common language that enables the team to talk intelligently about their ministry. Knowing what is involved in healing ministry enables teams to consciously give shape to their ministry. As the team reflects upon its ministry, the members help one another to grow in gifts and ability to minister.

Prayer by a team is a valuable resource in ministering to hurting Christians, but it is not easy; it requires skill developed by training. The next chapter describes how the cycle of ministry can give shape to a team's ministry to a supplicant.

For Further Reading

1. *Healing as a Parish Ministry: Mending Body, Mind and Spirit,* by Leo Thomas, O.P. and Jan Alkire. Ave Maria Press, 1992.

2. *Praying for Healing: the Challenge* by Benedict Heron, OSB. Dorton, Longman & Todd Publisher (England), 1989.

Summary—Chapter 2

This chapter describes eight ingredients in team healing ministry:

1. Prepare the team
   A. Create a sacred space
   B. Prepare by prayer
   C. Discuss practical matters

2. Welcome the Supplicant
   A. Introductions
   B. Explain ministry
   C. Brief prayer

3. Listen
   A. To the supplicant
   B. To the Lord

4. Make an agreement about ministry

5. Become a worshipping community

6. Enter into the heart of worship/ministry

    A. Use the prayer of affirmation

    B. Pray in specific detail for healing

    C. Pray imaginatively

    D. Use touch, when appropriate

    E. Use sacramentals: oil, candles, blessed water, salt

7. Do closure

    A. Give thanks to God

    B. Review ministry with the supplicant

    C. Review practical arrangements

    D. Say good-bye

8. Debrief

For Your Reflection—Chapter 2

1. Recall this chapter's story of team ministry to Gloria. What do you think was the most helpful thing the team did with her? Did any part of their ministry make you feel uncomfortable?

2. Identify an occasion when you were helpful to a hurting child, friend, relative, neighbor or stranger. (It need not be explicit prayer ministry.) Reflect on what you did and compare it to the 8 ingredients in healing ministry. How many of the 8 ingredients did you use?

3. This chapter points out the strengths of ministering religious healing as a team. Read Mark 6:7-12. Why do you think Jesus sent out his disciples in pairs? What might have been the advantages and disadvantages?

3

The Cycle of Ministry

❖   ❖   ❖   ❖   ❖

Jane was the leader of a newly formed prayer team at St. Mary's Catholic church. She and her teammates, Sue and Pete, had completed training for team ministry and wanted to offer ministry once a week in their parish. Their pastor had given his full support, including announcing it in the parish bulletin.

After seeing several supplicants over a period of several weeks, a man named Larry approached Jane after Mass on Sunday and told her he had back problems. He wondered if prayer might help. Jane gave him an appointment for the coming week. The team expected that praying for Larry's back would be a simple task, but his physical problem turned out to be the tip of an emotional, spiritual and relational iceberg.

At their first meeting, Larry poured out his story to the team, beginning with the fact that until several years ago he had been a truck driver. An accident had severely injured his back. Ever since then he had been in constant pain, even though he had had good medical treatment, including surgery. He had not been able to work since the accident.

Larry's disability caused considerable financial stress on his family. Unemployment benefits had run out, huge medical bills remained unpaid, and the bank was threatening foreclosure on their house.

Larry also reported that his relationship with his wife had deteriorated as a result of his injury. He said his wife was tired of his being around the house all the time, especially since she had to care for many of his needs. His children complained that they couldn't have the things they used to have before his injury.

Listening to Larry convinced the team that he suffered badly from low self-esteem because he could not support his family. His father-in-law blamed him for the lowered standard of living of his daughter and grandchildren. He told Larry that if he was "a real man," he would get out and work, no matter what. This criticism stirred up in Larry memories of his childhood, where he had not done well in school and had been criticized severely by teachers and parents. Whenever he made a mistake or failed to perform well, they called him "dumb," "lazy" and "stupid." He said that as a child he had never been able to measure up to their standards, and now once again he couldn't measure up.

Larry responded to the team's loving listening and told them his fears. He was afraid to do the simplest household task because he might further injure his back and cause even more pain. He was afraid to go out of the house lest he slip and fall. He was so fearful that he could not bring himself to take advantage of a rehabilitation program available to him. This program would help him learn to cope with pain better and then prepare him for a new kind of work.

Larry told the team of his anger at the person who had caused the accident. With some embarrassment, he said he resented almost everyone connected with the accident in any way: the trucking firm for whom he had worked; the insurance company; the surgeons who had treated him. Encouraged by the team's acceptance of him, he admitted he even felt bitterness towards God for "doing this to me."

The team detected that Larry unconsciously enjoyed some of the benefits of being disabled. He liked being cared for; he liked the leisure to read and to pursue his hobby of shortwave radio. He clearly wanted less pain but it was not clear whether he wanted to be completely healed of his injury.

After Larry finished telling his story, the team just sat in silence, feeling completely overwhelmed with his difficult situation. Pete felt like they had been handed the mixed up pieces of three different jigsaw puzzles.

Not knowing what to do, Sue moved directly into praying for Larry's injured back, then Pete prayed for his relationship with his wife, then Jane urged him to forgive all those who had hurt him. They moved quickly from one thing to another until they had covered all the items they could remember. The team ended ministry by telling Larry to come back the next week.

At the next session, in response to their questions about any improvement, Larry said nothing seemed to have changed. The team felt deeply disappointed, as they had expected him to report that healing had taken place. Still not knowing what to do, they essentially repeated the prayers of the first session. At the end of ministry they felt discouraged. In discussion, after Larry departed, the team decided they should "just turn it over to the Lord": they thought they had done all they could.

At their third meeting Larry still had no healing to report: his back pain persisted, his home life remained tense, he still felt angry. Convinced they had run out of options, the team told him that God always hears prayers; they had prayed in faith for his healing; and now he should "just claim his healing" and not "allow any negative thoughts to enter his mind." They did not schedule any further meetings with Larry. He politely thanked them for their trouble, but was obviously disappointed.

In their discussion after Larry left, everyone expressed discouragement. Jane and Pete thought they probably didn't have a gift of healing, while Sue thought Larry didn't have enough faith. The discussion degenerated into an argument, with the team members blaming each other for failing to heal Larry.

The failed ministry to Larry convinced everyone that they had no future as a team. They told their pastor they were discontinuing ministry because they didn't think God had really "called them" to healing ministry. But their pastor was unwilling to give up on the team as readily as they were giving up on themselves. Because Jane, Sue and Pete had been in our healing ministry training program, he asked them to talk to me before making a final decision.

When the team sat down with me, they told me about their ministry to Larry. Then Jane said they wanted my opinion about their decision to end ministering as a team. Looking at each discouraged face, I said I thought they might have reached the wrong conclusion. Instead of concluding that God was not calling them to healing ministry, I told them they had some learning to do and I was willing to help them with that learning. Initially the team expressed disappointment that I did not concur with their decision to stop ministry, but after some discussion they decided to accept my offer of help.

First, I said, they needed to contact Larry and offer to resume ministry with him. If he agreed to return, I would meet with the team weekly to help them learn how better to minister to him.

Larry accepted the team's offer. Before they met with him, we got together to review their assets. They had many positive qualities. The team had both sexes; all three members had been through the same training; they were ministering under the leadership of their pastor in their own parish. They truly wanted to serve the Body of Christ and were not on an ego trip. They were loving and had learned to listen well. (Their ability to listen had encouraged Larry to pour out his story freely.)

I then asked them to pinpoint their problem. They decided it was not knowing what to do with all the information Larry had given them. Also, the complexity of Larry's problems (the "mixed up pieces of three different jigsaw puzzles") had immobilized them. Each individual had responded with prayer but in a haphazard way, not as a unified team with a discernible plan.

The second session with Larry had been no different. The team still had no plan for ministry. Frustrated at the end of the second session, they adopted a super-spiritual stance in their ministry to Larry ("just turn it over to the Lord"). This super-spiritual stance led them, in the third session, to put the blame onto Larry for lack of healing ("claim your healing"). Blaming each other and deciding to quit their ministry out of a sense of failure were easy solutions for them at that point.

Fortunately, the team's pastor handled this wisely and would not accept their decision to abandon ministry without further discernment. Ceasing ministry would have deprived the church of a valuable resource and jeopardized each team member's spiritual life by ignoring God's call.

What the team needed with Larry was a systematic way of doing their ministry. I asked Pete how he started putting a jigsaw puzzle together. He said he did the edges first, then an area of one color such as the sky. I told the team they needed some similar plan and suggested we review the notion of Cycle of Ministry (which they had already studied in their training program) as a way of getting started in ministry with Larry.

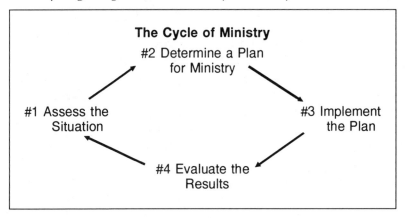

Figure 3

The diagram in Figure 3 shows the sequence of steps or phases of ministry. The Cycle of Ministry is actually a familiar process that everyone uses in everyday occurrences without being conscious of the fact.

For instance, suppose your child is playing in the back yard with some friends. Suddenly you hear screams and cries of distress. Rushing out to see what is wrong, you find your child screaming on the ground, entangled in her overturned tricycle. The first thing you will do is to assess the situation. Are any bones broken? Has she suffered a concussion? Or is she frightened? Or maybe angry? By looking and listening you discover she was pushed off her tricycle by a playmate and is furious. She has a skinned knee and badly bruised feelings. You have assessed the situation. This is step #1 of the cycle of ministry.

How do you help a child with a slightly skinned knee and badly bruised feelings? Certainly a band-aid and a kiss; probably a chance for her to tell you how angry she is with her playmate; and perhaps a glass of milk and a cookie while she has some time alone with you. Out of these possibilities you devise a plan of action. This is step #2 of the cycle of ministry.

So you take your child in the house; apply the band-aid; hold her while she tells you what she thinks of her playmate; give her several kisses and hugs; and supply her with a cookie and glass of milk. You have implemented your plan. This is step #3 of the cycle of ministry.

You notice your child has stopped crying, is climbing down from the table and says she wants to go out to play. You conclude that the problem is finished and that you can return to washing the dishes. You have evaluated the results of your ministry. This is step #4 of the cycle of ministry.

But if after the band-aids, cookies and hugs she still is whimpering and clinging on to you, your evaluation would be that something more is needed. The cycle would begin again. You would return to step #1 and reassess the situation. Perhaps she is overtired and cranky. You develop a new plan of action—put her down for a nap—which you implement. If she is her usual self after the nap you evaluate your plan of action as successful, and the event is finished.

The cycle of ministry is indeed a natural helping tool that we use in everyday life. But unless we make it a conscious process, identifying each step and giving them names, we will forget to use it in situations that are complex and bewildering. Then we become overwhelmed. It might be quite different if upon hearing your child's screams you discover that she has wandered into the street and has been struck by a truck and is bleeding profusely. You might very well panic and not be able to do anything helpful. The paramedic, on the other hand, has been trained to use the cycle of ministry approach even in the face of serious trauma and will automatically do so. We need to learn to do likewise in our ministry. The rest of this chapter describes the cycle of ministry, using Larry's case as an example.

Phase 1: Assessment

In the assessment phase we listen to the supplicant to determine what wounds we will minister to. I asked the team to review what Larry had told them in the first session, bearing in mind these questions:

- How has the supplicant's presenting problem affected the other dimensions of his life?
- What is the supplicant's core problem?
- How open is the supplicant to receive healing in these other dimensions?
- What are the supplicant's strengths and weaknesses?

As the team did this assessment, they saw that Larry's back injury had indeed affected the other three dimensions of his life. Emotional hurts from his past had been stirred up, his important relationships had suffered as a result of the injury, and he felt an inordinate anger and alienation from God.

Looking at the second question, the team thought that the physical injury was only the event that brought Larry's deeper, more vital problems to the surface. Even if he experienced a complete healing of his back, his other problems would remain, though in a less severe form. They suspected that the core problem was damaged self-esteem caused by a daily onslaught of criticism during childhood.

Examining the third question, the team concluded they did not know how open Larry was to receive ministry for these other wounds. This would have to be tested out by further conversation with him.

Finally, when pondering the last question, the team recognized two strengths in Larry. With the exception of his low self-esteem, his emotional life was basically healthy; and in spite of his present anger toward God, he was a deeply religious man.

I asked the team if they had been listening to God as they listened to Larry. Ministers sometimes receive information about a supplicant that seems to come from God. People "hear" God in many different ways. Some report that they hear an inner voice—not with their ears but with their mind. Others experi-

ence it like a thought that comes to them. Still others feel a
"hunch" that needs to be tested. The team said they were so
busy listening to Larry that they forgot to listen to God. If they
had remembered to do so, God might have revealed a deeper
reason why Larry was so angry and blaming so many people for
his troubles. Actually, without realizing it, the team may have
"heard" from God that Larry was ambivalent about receiving
complete healing.[1]

I told the team they had done a good job of making an
initial assessment. They had a good idea of the wounds that
were preventing Larry from being the person God intended him
to be. Also, they had some conjectures about the core problem.
Before moving into the next phase of the cycle of ministry (developing a plan of action), I reminded them of two facts about
assessment that they had learned in their training program:

1. Teams should not expect to make a complete assessment at
   the end of the first session. It gradually becomes clear as
   ministry continues.

2. Teams rarely can assess a situation until they can debrief
   alone. So during the first session the team needs to depend
   upon the leader's guidance of the prayer. This prayer can
   be of a general nature so that it does not commit the team
   to a permanent course of action. Affirmation prayer, prayer
   that God's love will engulf the supplicant, prayer that the
   supplicant will experience Christ's healing presence—all are
   valuable ways of praying in this first session, but do not pre-
   suppose a complete assessment has been made.

Phase 2: Determine a Plan of Action

Ordinarily the first decision for a team in determining a
plan of action is whether they are called to minister to this supplicant. This decision can be made by asking four questions:

---

1. What I'm describing here is a gift (charism) of knowledge, which I explain
more fully in Chapter 18.

1. Is prayer the proper way to bring healing to the supplicant's hurts? The St. Mary's team responded that since Larry was already receiving medical help, prayer seemed to be an appropriate remedy for his needs.

2. Do we have the time and energy to give the supplicant the ministry he needs? The St. Mary's team had no other supplicant, so they had no problem with time and energy.

3. Are we able to respect, love and have compassion for the supplicant? This team liked their supplicant, and there was much about him that they respected.

4. Are we, as a team, qualified to minister to the supplicant? The answer will depend upon the kind and severity of the supplicant's woundedness, and the team's talents, training, and experience. This was the only real question for St. Mary's team. Larry's hurts were complex, and the team was not very experienced. I led them through a discussion of their talents and training, and they decided that if I would continue to support them, they could minister to him. I agreed to meet with them for the next three weeks after each session with Larry. Although they were nervous, the team decided that with my support, they could minister to Larry.

   If a team decides it is not the team to minister, they must use great delicacy to communicate this to the supplicant and to help him get the ministry he needs.

The next item in formulating a plan of action is to define the need or needs that the team will minister to. Here again, several questions need to be asked:

1. What is the strategy for this particular ministry? Since a team cannot pray for a supplicant's every need, often they pray only for the explicit request. But sometimes a more basic wound needs to be healed before the explicit request can be met. The team must carefully explain this so that their supplicant does not feel unheard and uncared for.

   Another strategy is to pray for a need where there is the greatest likelihood of success. A small success in a significant area of a supplicant's life can have far-reaching effects. It can build her faith and overcome her feelings of hopelessness.

2. If more than one need exists, in what order shall they be addressed?

3. What needs *shouldn't* be prayed for? Every supplicant has more needs than any prayer team can possibly meet, so a team should not think it has to pray for every one of them. For some needs the team might make a referral. In Larry's case, the team might suggest that he and his wife make use of a marriage counselor. A referral would not mean that the team would not pray in any way for his marriage. The counseling might uncover the need for inner healing of wounds which are disrupting the marriage. Or the team might pray that God would empower the counselor to bring healing to this marriage.

I asked the St. Mary's team to formulate a plan of action for Larry in light of their assessment of his difficulties. They decided that in their first meeting, they would review with him the problems he had already shared with them, and then ask him for which of those he would like ministry. They would only pray for one need in this first session. And they would ask Larry to give them a lot of feedback as they ministered to him. They would encourage this by such statements as: "Tell us what are you experiencing as we pray;" "Tell us if you are feeling uncomfortable with what we are doing;" "Are you sensing anything that seems to be from God?" They would be prepared to follow up on his feedback.

I made several additions to the team's plan of action. I thought they needed to take up the issue of their having ended ministry prematurely. Second, I suggested they use prayer of affirmation at every reasonable opportunity. This would be healing to Larry's damaged self-image. Third, I proposed the team make frequent use of peaceful instrumental music, and that during the music they pray quietly for guidance from the Holy Spirit. They would receive this guidance by paying attention to the thoughts and images that came to them in this prayer time, and by discussing them as a team and with Larry when it seemed appropriate to do so. Fourth, I recommended that they not move to prayer for a new need until they had talked it over with Larry.

My most important addition to the team's plan was that they consciously foster love for Larry. They did not need to express it in words. They should spend a good amount of time praying with images that God's love would envelop Larry.

As we were ending our session, I said that in our next meeting I would want the team to report what happened as they implemented the plan of action.

Phase 3: Implement the Plan of Action

Much of what needs to be said about implementing the plan of action has already been covered in Chapter 2, and some of the resources available to prayer teams will be discussed in the next chapter. Here, I will note three difficulties teams experience in implementing their plan.

1. Teams do not always carry out the plan of ministry they have devised.

The logic of the cycle of ministry is that you assess the need, devise a plan to meet that need, and then actually carry out that plan. That seems simple and straightforward. But sometimes a team lacks the skill or knowledge needed to follow out its plan.

Even more often, a team fails to carry out their plan for ministry because they get distracted. As ministry progresses, the supplicant reveals new information about himself—new wounds or new reasons accounting for his woundedness. When this happens, the team should go back through the cycle of ministry—return to the assessment phase, reassess the need, revise the plan of action, if necessary, and then implement the revised plan.

Instead of going back through this cycle of ministry, however, teams tend to become fascinated with some aspect of the new information. Then, without going through the cycle of ministry, they attempt to minister to this newly discovered need. But before this new one is healed, they get fascinated with still another and so on. I call this "chasing rabbits." A dog chasing rabbits sometimes spies a second rabbit before he captures the first. He leaves the first one's trail and starts chasing the new one. The usual result is one exhausted dog with no captured rabbits.

2. Teams forget the original plan of action.

This may seem strange, but remember that ministry frequently extends over many weeks. So the team—and even the supplicant—can easily forget the original plan. They then gradually drift into a new plan or minister to new needs without even being aware they are doing so. The team leader needs to keep the plan of action firmly in mind and not let the team get distracted or forgetful.

3. The team lacks commitment.

This is the worst reason for not implementing the plan of action. When ministry extends over a long time, the team can become weary or bored with the process and just quit. They forget the loving commitment of fidelity they have made to the supplicant. Usually they find some excuse to end ministry prematurely. This damages the supplicant. It reinforces her sense of hopelessness, and is usually experienced as rejection.

The St Mary's team had never devised an explicit plan of action, but their implicit plan was that a single prayer for every need mentioned would bring immediate healing. When that did not happen, the frustrated team prematurely quit the ministry with Larry.

I met with the team the day after the first session of their renewed ministry to Larry. This time they came with smiles and excitement. Jane said the first thing they did was discuss with Larry their abrupt termination of ministry. She said he had blamed himself for the failure to achieve healing. Telling himself he had "blown it again," he had decided that he was hopeless and that even God had given up on him. So he was glad that the team was going to give him another chance. Jane said Sue had wept and asked his forgiveness for ending ministry just when he needed them most. Then Jane had led Larry and the team through a discussion of their feelings about their hasty decision. It settled the feelings of both Larry and the team and helped them re-establish rapport.

Jane then moved them into implementing the new plan for this first session. They reviewed with Larry the problems he had shared with them as they remembered it and then asked him where he would like to start ministry. To their surprise, he said he thought they should start with inner healing: with the childhood experience of never being able to measure up. He had come to this decision as a result of the discussion about his feelings of not measuring up to the team's expectation of immediate healing of his many problems.

Having agreed upon a plan to focus on inner healing for Larry's feelings of never living up to people's expectations, the team started praying. They began with a generous amount of praise using music and song. They had a deep sense of God's presence. They then used the prayer of affirmation generously. Larry began to sob. In response to their invitation to share what was happening, he told them that he experienced God himself affirming him. For the first time in his life he felt God's approval.

The team stayed with this experience for a long time. Using imagery, they prayed for God's love to envelop Larry. They also spent time silently loving Larry. Pete reported an image of God as Grandfather, holding Larry as a child on his lap and rejoicing in him as only a grandparent can do. This led the team to begin praying for healing of his childhood experience of being ridiculed for not "measuring up."

The team asked Larry to remember some particularly painful experience of being ridiculed. After a minute Larry began to cry. He remembered the day he had brought home a report card with a failing grade in English composition. His father had made him wear a dunce cap at the dinner table and berated him for being the family "dummy." From then on, his brothers and sisters called him Dummy when they wanted to tease him. He would lash out in anger, then his father would punish him for his temper. The team told Larry to invite Jesus into this scene. He did so and had a powerful experience of Jesus turning the whole scene around, healing his hurts and bringing reconciliation to the family members.

At the end of the hour both Larry and the team were completely exhausted but joyful. Jane asked Larry, "Was anything we did tonight especially helpful?" Larry said the most helpful thing was the team's request to give them feedback as they ministered to him. He had thought to himself that they must think he had something valuable to contribute to this prayer for healing or they wouldn't be asking him for feedback. He added that the team's affirmation of his feedback gave him confidence to believe that his experiences of God were real.

Since our conversation was sliding into an evaluation of the team's ministry I suggested that we consciously move into a discussion of the fourth phase of the cycle of ministry.

Phase 4: Evaluation of Ministry

Even while in the midst of actively implementing our plan for ministry we are constantly evaluating it. In the back of our minds we have such questions as:

- Is this ministry producing the intended results or not? If not, why not?
- Is it doing something we had not intended? Is this good or bad?

At certain points in ministry a more deliberate and conscious evaluation needs to be made. For example, a short time of evaluation should take place at the end of each session with the supplicant and later by the team alone during debriefing. A longer period of evaluation with the supplicant is necessary after the scheduled number of sessions have occurred. An evaluation is called for when the goals for ministry set at the beginning seem to have been reached, or when progress seems to have halted. The following questions can help in evaluation:

- How does the supplicant define the need for which he seeks ministry?
- How does the team define the need for which the supplicant is seeking ministry?
- What has the team done in response to the supplicant's request for help?
- What have been the results of this ministry, and how successful does the team judge it to have been?
- What part of the need remains unmet? What action does the team intend to take to meet the unmet need?
- What natural skills and talents, what virtues, what charisms have been most useful in this ministry? Where does God seem to have been most present in the ministry, and where most absent?

After answering the above questions, pray for strengthening the weaknesses and deficiencies, asking God to give all that is needed to minister to this supplicant. In concluding the evaluation phase, give praise and thanks to God for what he has done in this ministry.

To move the St. Mary's team into a time of explicit evaluation I asked them to rate their ministry to Larry using a scale of 1 to 10. Sue immediately placed it at 10, Pete thought 9, and Jane said 8 or 9. I then took them through a standard check list (see chapter summary) and asked them to note what they had done well and what they done poorly or forgotten to do. They had been deficient in only a few items: They had been so nervous before meeting Larry that they had not prepared very well. And they had been so excited at the end that they had not given clear instructions to Larry about future meetings. Nor had they done well in debriefing after Larry left. However, I told them their ministry as a team was off to an excellent start.

Evaluation is the best of all possible ways to learn. It is learning by reflecting upon one's own experience. If done frequently enough in planned and formal ways, it will become so habitual that ministry will always be a learning experience. Evaluation, then, enables ministers to grow in their ability to be an instrument of God's healing power.

Although he did not use the word "evaluation," this, in fact, was what the Pastor of St. Mary's suggested to the team when they wanted to disband. When they came to me, the first thing we did was evaluate their ministry. Through this process they discovered what their ministry lacked, decided it could be remedied, and so resumed their ministry to Larry. If they had not used this phase of the ministry cycle their ministry would have been lost to the church.

"Trust the Process"

I met with the St. Mary's team two more times. After that, they felt confident enough to continue ministry to Larry without my help. About a year after our last meeting, Jane reported to me the outcome of their ministry with Larry. They had met with him a total of eight times, not counting the first three before they came to me. About a year after their first meeting, Larry asked if he could meet formally with the team on the anniversary of their first meeting. Larry brought each of them a card with a personal message and a small gift. He thanked them for what they had done for him and his family, and asked if together they could offer a prayer of thanks to God.

Larry enumerated the benefits of their ministry. He said when the team concentrated on prayer for inner healing, his sense of never measuring up gradually subsided. Toward the end of the prayer ministry, he and his wife had entered marriage counseling and their relationship now was "just great." Larry had gone to a financial counselor and had taken advantage of the rehabilitation program available to him. As a result, he now had a steady job as an electronics repairman for a computer firm. He said his back never completely healed, but he went to a pain clinic and learned to handle the pain better. It didn't bother him much anymore.

Larry said the best thing that had happened to him was his relationship with God. Everyday he felt God's love and care for him and his family. Jane told me that Larry's concluding words were, "I'm a changed man: I'm a living miracle."

I asked Jane what she thought had been the most important thing the team had learned through their experience with Larry. She said that in one of their meetings with me I had said, when talking about the cycle of ministry, "Trust the process: when you don't know where you are going, follow the cycle of ministry and the steps to be taken in praying for healing." (The latter is listed in Chapter 2.) In fact, the team wrote the cycle of ministry and steps of prayer ministry on small cards for each team member. For a long time they kept them before them during ministry.

Jane said "trust the process" had become a slogan for them. They wanted to have every step made clear to them before even beginning ministry, but they knew that was impossible. The team now believed that God would lead them step by step. And they had to take each step in faith that it would lead to the next step. "That," said Jane, "is what 'trust the process' means for us."

Conclusion

Healing is a step-by-step process, not a one-time event. We (both teams and supplicants) enter into the process of the cycle of ministry without knowing its outcome. The cycle of ministry requires faith that God abides in us and works through us. "Trust the process" actually means trusting in the One who leads His people on a journey towards wholeness.

Teams that recognize and use the cycle of ministry discover that their ministry is focused and effective. God uses order, structure and time to bring healing to a wounded world.

For Further Reading

1. *Pastoral Care Emergencies*, by David Switzer. Paulist Press, 1989.

Summary—Chapter 3

Phase 1: Assessment

1. What is the supplicant's presenting (initial) problem?

2. How has the supplicant's presenting problem affected other dimensions of his life?

3. What is the supplicant's core problem?

4. How open is the supplicant to receive healing in these other dimensions?

5. What are the supplicant's strengths and weaknesses?

Phase 2: A Plan of Action

1. Are we called to minister to this supplicant? The following questions can help determine the answer:

   a. Is prayer the proper way to bring healing to the supplicant's hurts?

   b. Do we have the time and energy to give the supplicant the ministry he needs?

   c. Are we able to respect, love and have compassion for the supplicant?

   d. Are we as a team qualified to minister to this person?

2. What is the need or needs the team will minister to? Here again, several questions can help:

   a. If there is more than one need, in what order shall they be addressed?

   b. What needs *shouldn't* be prayer for?

   c. What is the strategy for this particular ministry?

Phase 3: Implementing the Plan of Action

If difficulties are encountered, these questions can help:

1. Is the agreed-upon plan of ministry being carried out?

2. Has the original plan been forgotten?

3. Does the team lack commitment to this supplicant?

Phase 4: Evaluation of Ministry

1. How has the supplicant defined the need for which he has sought ministry?

2. How has the team defined the need for which the supplicant has sought ministry?

3. What has the team done in response to the supplicant's request for help?

4. What have been the results of this ministry, and how successful does the team judge it to have been?

5. What part of the need remains unmet? What action does the team intend to take to meet the unmet need?

6. What natural skills and talents, what virtues, what charisms have been most useful in this ministry? Where does God seem to have been most present in the ministry, and where most absent?

7. After answering the above questions, it is useful to pray for strengthening the weaknesses and deficiencies, asking God to give all that is needed to minister to this supplicant.

8. In concluding the evaluation phase, give praise and thanks to God for what he has done in this ministry.

For Your Reflection—Chapter 3

1. This chapter describes healing ministry as a *process*, a sequence of steps that leads to healing. Review the summary of this chapter, then read Mark 8:22-25. How many of the phases of ministry do you see in Jesus' healing of this blind man? How many cycles of ministry did he need go through before the man could see clearly?

2. Recall an occasion when you attempted to be helpful to a hurting person, yet felt overwhelmed by the complexity of his/her situation. Fit your responses to the hurting person into the cycle of ministry. What phases in the cycle did you use? If you omitted any phase, envision how using it might have eased your feelings of stress and helped in your ministry.

3. Recall an occasion when you instinctively used the cycle of ministry to help a child, a friend, a relative or a stranger. How did the cycle help? What was the most helpful part of the cycle in this encounter?

4

Listening: A Divine Activity

❖   ❖   ❖   ❖   ❖

Mildred objected to my teaching. I was standing in front of sixty-five healing ministry students, stressing the importance of *listening* to the supplicant before praying for healing. I had just finished saying our responses either help or hinder the supplicant in telling us his story. Suddenly, from the middle of the room, Mildred interrupted. She said our course was supposed to teach people how to pray for "divine healing," but I was teaching "man-made techniques of counseling."

Silence followed Mildred's interruption. I wanted her to understand her dignity as a Christian, to know that her ministry makes Christ present to the suffering supplicant. What could help her grasp that pastoral listening is a divine activity as well as a human one?

I have learned that experience—even the experience of role-playing—will teach when words fail. So I asked Mildred if she would be willing to role-play a situation. When she agreed, I invented a script for her:

She would be "Mary," an unmarried, 22-year-old woman from a small town, now in a big city. She had been working as a sales representative for a big advertising agency—her first important job. Her boss, Dan, had taken a special interest in Mary, helping her learn her way around in the advertising world and in the social scene. This relationship developed into an affair, but Dan made it clear he was committed to his marriage even though he was cheating on his wife.

The event Mildred would role-play would be Mary's responses to a medical examination that shows she is pregnant by Dan. Mary has told Dan, who has reacted with anger, telling her to get an abortion. I told Mildred she should play Mary as being very upset, not wanting an abortion, but not seeing any other way out and not knowing where to turn for help. Mildred's partner in the role-play would be Irene, a woman who was teaching with me. She would play the part of Mary's roommate, "Jane." Mary has turned to Jane with her problem, hoping for an answer. Irene's script described Jane as being religious, but self-righteous and moralistic—a woman who loves Mary but disapproves of her lifestyle and wants her to be more religious. The role-play would start in Mary and Jane's apartment the evening Mary has found out about her pregnancy.

"Hi, Mary. How was your day?"

(Mary sighs deeply.) "I didn't have a good day. I didn't go to work. I went to the doctor instead."

"What's wrong?"

(Mary again sighs deeply; long pause.) "I'm pregnant!"

(Jane, with obvious shock): "You're *what?* . . . Mary, I told you you were playing with fire. And now you've gotten burnt."

"Don't scold me, Jane. I thought I could count on you. I'm hurting—bad."

"I can see that, and you can count on me. I'm here. I want to help. And I'm listening, but I'm shocked."

(Mary, angrily): "I didn't expect you to be shocked. I'm in a tight spot. I expected you to have some feelings about *me.*"

"I do. I really love you. I feel bad about this . . . But I thought you were smarter than to get in a mess like this."

"You're supposed to be my 'friend.' Forget it. I don't want to talk anymore about it. I really needed someone

to talk to. But I guess I'm going to have to go it alone.
I'm leaving."

"Where are you going to go? You need help. You stay
right here and talk to me. What are you going to do
about the baby?"

"That's the problem. Dan says if I don't have an abortion, he'll fire me. I can't have a baby with no money
and no job. And I can't tell my parents. It would kill
them."

"I'm ashamed of you for even thinking of murdering
your baby! How can you expect God to help you if you
commit that sin? I think it's about time that we pray
about this. You need to ask God's pardon. Then
maybe he'll give you a way out."

"A big help you are! I'm hurting, I'm scared, and I
come to you because you're religious. I thought you
would help me. But all you're interested in is saving my
soul. Forget it. I'm leaving." (Mary angrily gets up and
leaves.)

Following the role-play, Mildred said she was amazed at the
effect the simulation had upon her. As she had heard her script
for the role-play, she had felt tears welling up. As she acted the
part of Mary, she felt a desperate need to pour her heart out and
was hoping Irene would play the role of Jane in a loving way. In
the role-play she felt frightened, confused and cornered. She
was amazed that she felt genuine anger at the way "Jane" talked
to her. Mildred said she could not believe she was being treated
in such an unloving way. But even so, when Jane made more
offers to help, she tried again to be heard. Finally she wasn't
willing to talk, let alone pray, with Jane. By the end of the role-
play, Mildred said she felt deeply betrayed by "Jane."

This role play illustrates a mistake—both serious and frequent—that ministers make: They pray with supplicants before
listening deeply to their story. The result is that the ministers
don't know what God has been doing in their supplicant's life
and what areas have not yet been touched by God. So they pray

badly. But even if they are on target, supplicants usually do not experience God's presence because they do not feel they have been heard by God through the team's listening.

Ministers who do not listen have failed to realize that Christian listening is more than a human skill. When done "in Christ" it is a divine activity, based upon faith and exercised in love. "Jane" had an established relationship with "Mary." She loved her roommate and had her welfare at heart. But she failed in the most crucial task of a helper: to establish a *healing* relationship. How does one do this? I believe the answer to this question is so important that it needs to be answered from two points of view: the psychological and the religious. This chapter addresses the question from a psychological standpoint. The next chapter will answer it from a pastoral care position.

Qualities of a Healing Relationship

In the early 1960's two psychologist, Traux and Carkhuff[1], stated that three qualities are indispensable for a healing relationship: accurate empathy, non-possessive warmth and genuineness.

Accurate Empathy

Empathy is the ability to know what it feels like to be *this* person in *this* situation. It is the ability to get "into the skin" of another. Without being aware of it, most people use empathy naturally in everyday situations. For example, a kindergartner comes downstairs to breakfast complaining that he feels too sick to go to school today. His mother touches his forehead, observes him carefully, listens to his tone of voice and decides something other than sickness is going on. She responds by saying:

> "That's too bad. Are you going to miss anything important at school today?"

---

1. Traux, C. and Carkuff, R.R., *Toward Effective Counseling and Psychotherapy*, Chicago, Aldine Publ. Co., 1967.

The child responds, "No, just a dumb old tasting party. We're going to taste artichokes."

The mother says, "And you hate artichokes don't you? Would it help if I wrote a note to the teacher saying you didn't have to taste them?"

The child smiles, says "Yeah," then admits he might be well enough to go to school after all.

The mother accurately understood what it felt like to be *this* child facing *this* unpleasant situation and not knowing how to handle it. Empathy is an everyday matter for a parent. Of course, some have it naturally to a greater degree than others, but empathy can be learned and developed.

Jane had no empathy for Mary in her situation because she had her own agenda.[2] She wanted to make Mary understand that her behavior had been wrong and had brought this consequence as a punishment. ("I told you you were playing with fire, and now you've gotten burnt.") Also, Jane wanted to keep Mary from compounding the mistake by having an abortion. ("I'm ashamed of you for even thinking of murdering your baby!") Jane's personal agenda prevented her from feeling how cornered and trapped Mary felt. Because Mary did not experience being understood, she was not open to Jane's solutions.

Non-Possessive Warmth

To be truly helpful, we must love supplicants with *agape* love, the kind of love with which God loves us. Scripture scholar William Barclay defines *agape* love as "invincible goodwill, unconquerable benevolence." God refuses to treat us as an enemy. He loves us even in our sinfulness. God does not make us earn his love.

The psychological term "non-possessive warmth" is related to *agape* love. As a Christian minister, I love supplicants with

---

2. For more on the problem of pursuing one's own agenda, see Chapter 7 of *Healing as a Parish Ministry*. The chapter describes eight pitfalls of ministry, including their major symptoms and the spirituality needed to avoid these problems.

God's love; I love them just as they are. They do not need to act
or talk in a way to earn my love. I do not love supplicants on
condition that they give up their sin. Of course in desiring the
very best for them, I hope they will give up sinful ways, but I do
not withhold my love until they do so.

Jane couldn't show this kind of warmth to Mary. Undoubt-
edly she felt what many people do—that if she was "soft" on her,
she would not give up her sin. She was trying to coerce Mary
into being good. This is not God's way. God calls, challenges
and points out the consequences of sin, but God does not coerce.

Genuineness

To be genuine means to be one's true self with another person, not phony but also not a blank wall, withholding one's self.
A genuine person does not assume an artificial role with the
other. Jane apparently felt compelled to be both judge and
prosecutor for Mary. She did not allow herself to be just Jane, a
friend to her roommate in a time of need. Her failure to
achieve the three qualities of a healing relationship meant that
her conversation with Mary was destructive rather than healing.

Listening Deeply Promotes Healing

Even though the role play was finished, Mildred still seemed
upset. I mentioned this and she agreed, saying she knew that
Irene was just playing a role and following directions in her
script, but Mildred was still angry with her. She felt uncared for
and couldn't seem to let go of the role. The class was having
similar feelings, so I suggested we repeat the role-play, only this
time with the listener taking a helpful rather than a hurtful
stance. Mildred and the class liked the idea, and Mildred agreed
to play the same role again. Leonard, a staff member, agreed to
play the listening stance.

Leonard's script was to play Mary's favorite uncle Ed, a
priest who had frequently visited Mary's family as she was growing up. Mary and Ed had always been fond of one another. As

she had grown older, she occasionally consulted her uncle on religious questions. I instructed Leonard to display the three qualities of a helping relationship. "Ed" would listen carefully and be as helpful as possible. The scene would start with them seated in his office.

After a few chatty remarks about her family, Uncle Ed says:

"Mary, I got the impression in our telephone call that you have something serious to discuss."

"Yes. I don't know anyone else to talk to. I'm scared. I don't know what to do."

"You sound desperate. Can you tell me about it?"

"Well, when I first came to the city, it was all new to me. I'd never been in a big city before. I tried really hard to get a good job so my parents would be proud of me. So I got this job in the advertising agency, but I didn't know which way was up. My boss Dan was really good to me. He showed me the ropes. He introduced me to the right people and to some good clients." (Mary stops and looks down at her hands.)

"It must be hard for you to talk to me about this."

"Yes. I'm not very proud of what I've done. See, we started going out together. He's married, but somehow I closed my eyes to that, even though he told me he was committed to his marriage. Well, you can guess that one thing led to another. I went to the doctor today and he said I'm pregnant." (Tears run down Mary's cheeks.)

"That must be a shock to you."

"I just can't believe it. I can't believe it's happening to me. . . . I can't talk to my folks about it. They'd be so upset. (sobs) And I called Dan at work and he told me I'd better have an abortion."

"How do you feel about that?"

"I'm in a state of shock. I . . . I . . . just can't believe he would . . ." (Her voice trails off.)

"He's not willing to take any responsibility for the baby?"

"Just pay for the abortion is all. But I guess what hurts the most is that he is really telling me to get lost. He didn't even want to talk to me about it. Well, now I don't want to talk to him either! I don't know what I want to do—just run away, I guess. But I've got no place to run to."

"You're feeling pretty confused?"

"Yes, I don't know what to do. I don't have any options. What will I do if I have this baby? I can't go back to work there. I don't have any money. I can't support this baby. How can I work and care for a child? How can I be a mother to this child with no father around? I don't know what to do."

"It looks pretty bleak."

(Mary sighs) "Yeah." (Long pause.)

"You've said several times that you don't have any options. Let's look at that for a few minutes. I want to look at who and what can be of help to you. You said you couldn't tell your folks. Is that really true?"

(Long pause, then Mary sighs) "Well . . . I don't know. I'm afraid they're going to get real mad."

"What do you fear most about telling them?"

"Oh, I don't know. (Pause) I'm afraid they're going to tell me that I'm no good. Going off to the city and getting pregnant. You know. Maybe they'll say I'm trash. They probably won't ever trust me again."

"Are you willing to risk that by telling them?"

"Maybe . . . if you were there . . . if you were there, maybe they wouldn't get so angry with me. Would you help me tell them?"

"Yes. I'd be willing to be there when you tell them. The reason I'm suggesting that you tell them is that you need all the help you can get. They will feel bad, but I know them well enough to think they will stick by you. Do you have anyone else you can talk with and depend on?"

(Mary pauses, thinking.) "Yes. I have one friend I can count on."

"Good. I suggest you call her up and see if you can stay with her tonight. We'll talk to your parents tomorrow. But first, I'd like to check out one thing with you. I gather that you don't want an abortion but you just don't know what to do if you have the baby. Is that right?"

"Yeah, just the mention of abortion horrifies me. But I just don't know anything about being a mother."

"It's a big responsibility, all right, but this is not the time to make important decisions. You're still in a state of shock. You're confused and scared. Our first task is to find all the support for you that we can. The more important decisions can come later. Is there anything more we need to do today?"

"Uncle! Would you say a prayer for me that I will do the right thing?"

"I'd be glad to. Let's do that together, right now."

In the discussion following the role-play, Mildred said that in playing Mary she had learned how cornered a woman in Mary's situation feels. She said that *helpless, hopeless,* and *alone* described what she felt. She said she had learned the importance of being heard in Mary's situation. The feeling of aloneness was so gripping that it even excluded God's presence. She said, "I'd put it this way: my head couldn't think, even to pray, until my heart had been heard and someone had reached out to help me." As she played the role of Mary the first time, it got worse and worse, as though God were rejecting her.

In the second role-play, Mildred's feelings of helplessness, hopelessness and aloneness gradually dissolved as "Uncle Ed" listened. Finally it seemed as though God had heard her and had reached out to her. Only then could she think of prayer and of doing "the right thing." Until then, all her energies had been taken up in self-preservation.

After this role-play, Mildred was able to get out of the role of Mary. She could leave Mary's feelings behind and be Mildred again. The class, too, was relieved. Since the purpose of the role-plays had been to demonstrate the need to learn the principles of holding a healing, pastoral conversation, I asked Mildred to tell us what had been helpful and unhelpful in the second role-play.

Regarding empathy, Mildred thought that Uncle Ed had been quite accurate in knowing how cornered, confused, and hopeless Mary felt. His understanding of how she felt enabled Mary to continue telling her story even when she found it embarrassing.

In regard to non-possessive warmth, Mildred gave Uncle Ed high marks. She said that although Mary knew that her uncle did not approve of her adulterous relationship, she never felt he was condemning her. Furthermore, although Mary knew her uncle did not want her to have an abortion, she never felt coerced by him as she had with Jane. Mildred said that, as Mary, she never felt she had to win her uncle's love. It was just there, no matter what she did or said.

As to genuineness, Mildred thought Ed came across as genuine. He did not "play games" with Mary; he did not assume an artificial role. He was just himself—a priest-uncle who dearly loved his niece and wanted the best for her.

As we ended the discussion of the two role-plays, Mildred said she thought she was beginning to believe that I was teaching more than "man-made" counseling techniques. But she still found it hard to believe that her listening could be a divine activity. I agreed that it is hard, but it is true.

For Further Reading

1. *Health Care Ministers*, by Nancy McGee. Winston Press, 1982.

Summary—Chapter 4

A. This chapter describes what pastoral listening is:

    1. *Pastoral listening is a divine activity.* It is more than a human action. Ministers of Christ's healing love listen to a wounded member of his Body. Out of love, they listen in faith and in hope.

    2. *Pastoral listening is purposeful.* Ministers listen so that supplicants may experience God as a listening God, They listen so that they may know how to minister healing to supplicants' hurts.

B. An effective pastoral listener brings three psychological qualities to a relationship:

    1. *accurate empathy:* the ability to know what it feels like to be *this* supplicant in *this* situation.

    2. *non-possessive warmth:* unconditional, agape love

    3. *genuineness:* being oneself with another person.

C. In pastoral listening the minister is actively involved in helping supplicants tell their story. (The next chapter describes this active involvement.)

For Your Reflection—Chapter 4

1. Recall a time when you found someone to listen to you, just when you desperately needed a good listener. What did s/he do that was especially helpful to you? Looking at the three qualities of a good listener (in the chapter summary), how many of these qualities did you experience in that encounter?

2. Who is the best listener you know? In what ways has his/her listening helped you? Has this person helped you experience God as a listening God?

3. Reflect on your ability to listen to others. On a scale of 1 to 10, how would you rate yourself? In which of the three qualities of a good listener are you strongest? In which of the three qualities do you need the most growth? End this reflection question by thanking God for the listening skills you already have. Ask God to give you the gift of listening in those areas where you think you need some growth.

4. Read Psalm 139:1-6, then reflect on how you experience God listening to you. What are the different ways God answers you? How do you listen to God?

5

Characteristics of a Good Pastoral Listener

❖　　　❖　　　❖　　　❖　　　❖

The first role-play in the last chapter ends with "Mary" angrily storming out of the room, unhelped by her roommate. Unless she finds someone else to help her, she probably will have an abortion. In the second role-play, Mary ends up praying with her priest-uncle that she will do the right thing; she probably will not have an abortion. What made the difference? This chapter answers this question by describing the characteristics of a good listener from a pastoral care point of view. It shows how a listener can respond helpfully to a supplicant's story, and points out some important helps and obstacles to good listening.

Good listening is rare. Recall an occasion in which you tried to share with another your deepest feelings about something very important to you. Unless you were unusually fortunate, your listener quickly became disinterested and restless, and soon butted in with a concern of her own. She probably started telling you of something similar that happened to her, or she may have simply changed the subject. In short, she did not display the personal qualities of a good listener.

Personal Qualities of a Good Listener

1. Self-sacrifice

Attentive listening demands a great deal of self-sacrifice. It requires that we restrain our desire to tell *our* story. This is a sacrifice because listening to another's anguish stirs up memories of our own experiences which we have never shared with another. It's hard to put aside our own painful feelings and share in a supplicant's suffering. Or, if someone is telling us about her joys, we may find envy rising up within us if we do not have this joy in our life.

To be a good listener, we must share in people's pain and rejoice over their good fortune. Learning to listen is really learning to love, which means following the One who said, "I have come in order that you may have life—life in all its fullness. I am the good shepherd, who is willing to die for the sheep." (TEV, Jn 10:10b-11)

2. Respect

Another characteristic of a good listener is the ability to respect the supplicant. Only when we respect another will our listening be healing. Yet in the ministry of religious healing, we sometimes are called upon to minister to people who repel us. We can still minister effectively if we can respect *some* aspect of a supplicant's life.

Dolly was especially hard for me to like. When she came to me for help, she was pregnant by someone other than her husband, with whom she was still living. She was never clean, had a fierce temper and was filled with hatred for people in general, which she expressed with foul language. Initially I found her so unpleasant that I thought I couldn't minister to her. But as I thought more about her, I discovered I could respect her intense desire to be a better person in the face of overwhelming obstacles. This degree of respect enabled me to listen with empathy to Dolly. I came to know what it was like to be someone overwhelmed by a world too complex for her to understand. Healing came to her from my listening.

3. Unconditional love

To listen well to someone, we must give up the need for supplicants to behave, think or talk according to our expectations. Instead, we must love others with Christ's love, a love that is free of conditions. Unconscious ideals influence our feelings about the other person when he does not conform to our standards of behavior.

Dolly did not meet my standards. She was not clean; she used foul language; she was sexually promiscuous. I had to restrain my desire to reject her for these traits. To learn what it was like to be Dolly, I had to set aside my demand that she conform to my standards.

4. Serenity

Good listening requires serenity. Yet listening deeply to another sometimes makes us anxious. Prayer is a good way to handle this. It focuses our attention upon Christ, who gives us peace. A period of prayer prior to ministry can help. Silent prayer while listening to a supplicant can aid in maintaining serenity. The silent prayer should be simple so that it will not distract us from listening, e.g., silently saying the name of Jesus. A conscious awareness of Jesus' presence dispels anxiety.

Helpful Responses

Our responses have the power to help or hinder a supplicant's telling of his story. Good, active listening can be done with a few kinds of responses. Each has its own purpose.

1. Indications of Acceptance

Our responses to a supplicant should indicate our acceptance of the person and what she is telling us. Listeners often shy away from communicating acceptance because they think responding in an accepting way indicates approval of the supplicant's opinion. But *acceptance is not the same as approval.*

Uncle Ed did not approve of Mary's behavior any more than did her roommate, Jane. But his responses let Mary know he accepted her and wanted to understand how she viewed her problem. His acceptance enabled Mary to continue telling her story. She never thought her uncle approved of her considering an abortion. On the other hand, Jane's immediate expressions of disapproval blocked her from finding out how Mary felt about her situation. Her condemnation isolated Mary and drove her towards abortion, not away from it.

Non-verbal ways to indicate acceptance include head nods, facial expressions, hand gestures and body postures. Verbal ways include "yes," "I see," "Uh-huh." These responses are so instinctive that we rarely notice we use them. But we need to become conscious of them so that we may use them purposefully.

2. Reflective Responses

A reflective response goes beyond a mere indication of acceptance. It says to the speaker what we have understood him to be telling us. This allows him to correct us if we have misunderstood. He may expand upon our statement if our understanding is incomplete. If we are "on target," he will continue his story, knowing we have understood so far.

When Mary said, "I went to the doctor today and he said I'm pregnant," Uncle Ed used a reflective response: "That must be a shock to you." Shock may not have been the best word to describe what Mary felt, but it was sufficiently accurate to encourage Mary to continue. She enlarged Uncle Ed's understanding by talking about her confusion, her fear of telling her folks, and her feelings of pressure from Dan to have an abortion.

3. Focusing Responses

A focusing response has two uses: First, it can help the supplicant keep on track with his story. Many people find it hard to tell their story in a straight-forward, concise way. When a person has lost track of the thread of his story, a focusing response gets him back on track.

For example, a supplicant tells of being sent to boarding school at an early age and experiencing this as rejection by her parents. As she tells the story, she starts reminiscing about sports at the boarding school. This leads her to talk about how much she loves sports. The listener, realizing the supplicant is off on a tangent, might say something like: "Let me interrupt here. You were telling me you experienced being sent to boarding school as rejection by your parents. I'd like to know a little more about your feelings of rejection."

A focusing remark can also be used to call a person back to an important point he has rushed over. Uncle Ed did this with Mary. During a pause after she had told the highlights of her story and expressed her feelings, he said, "You've said several times that you don't have any options." Then he said he wanted to look more closely at that statement. This helped Mary focus on who could help her. She decided her parents might help. She came to recognize that her uncle was a resource and that she could count on a close friend. Realizing she had these people to help her removed some of her feelings of helplessness and aloneness. She gained some sense of being in control once again. This stimulated her to start thinking of alternative solutions ("Uncle, would you say a prayer for me that I will do the right thing?").

Sometimes listeners find they need more information than the supplicant has given them, or they need to clarify something. A direct question can accomplish this. But direct questions need to be used sparingly because their over-use sets up an atmosphere of interrogation. This causes passivity in the supplicant and discourages her from telling her story as she wants to. Rapport suffers, the flow of dialogue is disrupted, and both listener and supplicant become frustrated. Instead of direct questions, an indirect approach usually works better, e.g., "Would you tell a little more about that?" or "I am not sure I understand what happened."

However, sometimes a direct question is the only sensible way to get needed information or clarification. For instance, after Mary said she feared telling her parents about her pregnancy, Ed used the direct question, "Are you willing to risk that by telling them?" He would have had difficulty getting that clarification any other way. His question actually was a way of asking her to make a decision. After Mary said Dan wanted her to have an abortion, Ed asked directly "How do you feel about that?" This was the simplest way to get that piece of information; it did not interrupt Mary's flow of telling her story.

4. Facilitating Responses

Sometimes, without being explicit, a supplicant says something that implies an important feeling, meaning, or conflict. Listeners need to openly acknowledge they have heard this, and make a response that encourages the supplicant to be explicit. These are called *facilitating* responses because they give the supplicant permission to talk about painful or embarrassing topics.

Uncle Ed used a facilitating response when Mary showed embarrassment as she started telling her story. He said, "It must be hard for you to talk about this." Mary said, "Yes, I'm not very proud of what I have done." This was a crucial point of the relationship between them. Rapport was at stake. But Ed's open recognition of her feelings enabled her to continue her story.

Uncle Ed might have made a facilitating response when Mary expressed anger about Dan: "Well, I don't want to talk to him either!" He could have said something like, "It sounds like you are pretty angry at him." This would have enabled Mary to talk more about her feelings toward Dan. However, Ed felt that in the current crisis, he needed to lead Mary out of her feelings of hopelessness. At some later time, she probably would need to talk out her feelings toward Dan.

Helps to Good Listening

We converse for many different purposes. Not all conversations strive to be healing, and not all listening attempts to be ministry. But if a conversation has healing as its goal, it must be structured to be effective. Structuring a conversation means consciously arranging the various elements according to a plan agreed upon by both minister and supplicant. For example, the conversation will take place in a determined setting, over a determined period of time, and for a specified purpose.

People often confuse structure with formality and rigidity. They are not the same. A pastoral conversation can be informal and flexible and still structured. The structure of listening resembles several of the ingredients in team healing ministry (described in Chapter 2):

1. Setting

The setting of a pastoral conversation is covered under "Prepare the Team" in Chapter 2. Here I'll emphasize that attentive listening demands a place that is quiet, private and protected from interruptions.

2. Time

The element of time is covered under "Make an Agreement about Ministry" in Chapter 2. Here I'll add that the formality of structure depends upon the situation. Time structuring in a family is less formal than that of a prayer team with a supplicant. But in both cases *some* structure is involved. A mother cooking an evening meal and approached by a small child who is crying needs to spend two or three minutes immediately, listening with full attention. The same woman cooking dinner and interrupted by a phone call from a supplicant would probably say, "I'm busy cooking dinner right now. May I call you back after we eat?" By responding this way, she structures the time element in a helpful way. Her first priority is to her family. She could not listen to the telephoning supplicant effectively, knowing she is neglecting her family. She would become irritated and the supplicant would not get her full attention. For effective ministry, there must be definite times designated for listening. No one can have a listening stance all the time.

People request ministry at inopportune times. We can use structuring responses to handle these. For example, Marge is getting ready to leave for a dentist's appointment. Jenny, a newly-wed who lives next door, comes bursting in the back door, sobbing. She says, "I have to talk to you right now. I'm so upset. Bob and I just had our first fight. I'm afraid he won't come home tonight. He might never come back! Would you call him up at the office and talk to him? Maybe he'll listen to you."

Marge spends a few minutes finding out that Bob became angry because Jenny would not get up and fix breakfast for him before he went to work. Then she says, "Jenny, I have ten minutes to get to a dentist appointment. But I'll be back about one o'clock and could talk to you then. Will that work for you? I'd be glad to say a short prayer with you before I leave."

Not only should there be a definite time for listening, but the length of time should be clearly stated. This is useful for both the speaker and the listener. The supplicant knows how much time he has and can pace his conversation accordingly. The listener can give his full attention to the supplicant without anxiety about how long the conversation will last.

For instance, when Jenny comes back at one o'clock, Marge might say, "I have an hour before the kids come home from school. I'll need to stop when they come home." Prayer teams can and should be more precise in setting a time for ministry, say on Wednesday from 2:00 to 3:00 p.m.

3. Expectations

Clarifying expectations is a form of making an agreement about ministry (Point #4 in Chapter 2). It's like making a contract with someone.

Jenny's behavior in seeking help from Marge illustrates the importance of clarifying each person's expectations of ministry. When she burst through Marge's kitchen door, she did not think of herself as asking for ministry. Nor had she reflected upon the appropriateness of asking Marge to intervene by phoning Bob. She was frightened by Bob's anger and was acting in panic. If Marge had allowed herself to be caught up in Jenny's anxiety, and neglected to clarify both of their expectations, the result would have been disappointment and frustration for each of them, plus ineffective ministry to Jenny.

A person requesting ministry always has expectations of how the team will help her. These expectations usually are vague, and the person seldom is conscious of them. The team also has expectations of the kind of help they are willing to give. These need to be clearly defined and made conscious because the team is responsible for working out a mutually acceptable agreement with the supplicant about the ministry to be given. Agreements should include the same points covered in Point #4, Chapter 2. Further clarification usually is needed as ministry proceeds.

Some supplicants' expectations of help conform to the team's. They want someone to listen to them, perhaps help them think of a solution, and usually pray with them. Others' have expectations of help that differ vastly from the team's. Jenny wanted Marge to phone her husband and straighten him out. Being a next-door neighbor, Jenny expected she could drop in any time she wanted for ministry. Marge had a different set of expectations about the help she was willing to give. She had other obligations and was only willing to do ministry at scheduled times. Jenny may have expected that Marge's ministry would be available to her as long as she lived next door. Marge would not want to foster Jenny's dependency upon her and would only be willing to minister to her for a limited period—say four or five times.

If Marge does not bring these differences into the open and come to some mutual agreement with Jenny, the ministry will likely end in conflict and hurt feelings. How can Marge do this? When Jenny returns in the afternoon Marge can help Jenny tell her story. She can then ask, "How can I be of help to you?" When Jenny says she wants Marge to call Bob and tell him not to be so demanding, Marge can respond that if she does that, Bob probably will feel that she is butting in and that Jenny has put her up to it. She can point out this would just make things worse. Then Marge could tell Jenny what she is willing to do: help Jenny think of how she can talk to Bob about the problem. If Jenny agrees that this will be helpful, Marge might then say, "I can see you tomorrow at one for an hour. If you need more time, I can see you three more times and then we'll look at how things are going. Is that agreeable to you?"

I remember myself as a young priest in a pastoral training program telling my advisor that it embarrassed me to talk about expectations with a supplicant: it made me seem cold and impersonal, and I wanted to appear friendly. My advisor responded, "If you don't love your supplicants enough to do what is right for them, you should quit being a minister." That was hard for me to hear, but it has been a guiding principle for me ever since.

The beginning minister often feels embarrassed about working out an agreement because in most social situations, we leave things vague. But that does not work in ministry. Working out details is a loving thing to do.

4. Confidentiality

The supplicant always expects confidentiality of the minister or team, even if she does not mention it. The team should take the initiative in discussing this expectation. They should explain their understanding of confidentiality and explicitly promise to maintain it. But even if it isn't promised, the team is nevertheless obliged to keep secret everything learned about the supplicant, or even about others, from the ministry.

Confidentiality is a sacred obligation. The information we receive during ministry is not ours to give away. It has been given to us as a sacred trust only because we are standing in the place of Jesus. We must not share it with friends or even with our spouses. We should not even disclose that someone has come to us for ministry.

Any violation of confidentiality is disastrous to the entire Body of Christ! It destroys trust not just in the ministry of the one who violates confidentiality, but causes distrust of *all* ministry. If people even suspect their confidence will be betrayed, they will be reluctant to seek ministry. This will deprive them of the abundant life that Jesus offers.

Obstacles to Good Listening

Listening can be hampered by two major obstacles: anxiety and misconceptions.

Anxiety can paralyze our effectiveness as listeners. Usually it arises from feelings of incompetence. For example Glenda, a beginning student in our training program, reported to me about her first experience of team ministry. She said she was so nervous during ministry that she started to sweat when the supplicant entered the room. That embarrassed her, so she became even more nervous and forgot his name as soon as he said it. While trying to remember what the team was supposed to say and do in the first session with the supplicant, she missed everything he said in the first few minutes.

Glenda knew she was supposed to listen, but she couldn't. She told me, "I was too worried. I kept thinking, 'What if the leader calls on me to pray for this man? What will I say? I don't even know what he wants prayer for!'" Finally she got hold of herself and started to pray silently. After awhile she calmed down enough to start to hear what the supplicant was saying. He had had tragic experiences in his childhood. The team leader was helping him tell his story. The leader didn't call on Glenda, but at the end of ministry, she was able to say a brief prayer, asking God to give the supplicant peace.

Glenda's experience is common for beginning ministers. In the presence of the supplicant, her self-confidence ebbed away. She felt awkward and unskilled. She couldn't remember what she had already learned. She worried about what she might be called upon to do. These anxieties prevented her from listening to the supplicant.

Everyone has these feelings in the beginning. The most effective remedy is experience. But even in this first session, Glenda was finally able to pray briefly. She remembered to pray silently and this calmed her. Being a member of a team gave her time to get a hold of herself. This is an important advantage of team ministry.

In discussing this experience with me, Glenda reduced her anxiety by reflecting on her ministry in a purposeful way. Through it, she began to learn what areas needed more attention. I pointed out abilities she couldn't see in herself. Thus she learned from her experience, became more skillful, and grew in confidence.

Misconceptions are the second obstacle to good listening. Often ministers experience their misconceptions as persistent thoughts—mental "tapes" that deafen them to what a supplicant is saying. Here are a few common ones:

1. *"I must straighten out this person."* In last chapter's first role-play, Jane was unable to listen because she thought her task was to "set Mary right" about moral issues.

2. *"I must solve this person's problem."* I experienced this with Marie, who came to me for ministry. She told me her daughter was going to give up her faith to marry a man who hated all religions. Marie wanted me to talk to her daughter, saying, "I know she would listen to you." Marie continued talking, but I was no longer hearing her. My thoughts were frozen. At first I felt something like panic, then dread, then anger. I caught myself about to say, "I have to go now, but let's pray about that." I knew I did not "have to go." What was happening?

Still unable to "hear" Marie, I restrained my impulse to terminate the session. I started to pray silently for God's guidance. I repeated the name of Jesus in rhythm with my breathing. Quickly my feelings subsided and I connected with Marie's story. All of this took less than a minute. I told Marie that I wished I could talk her daughter out of her decision, but I couldn't. She would resent my interference. It would only make matters worse. Instead, I proposed we explore what else I could do to help. Together we worked out a way that I could minister to Marie's needs.

Here, I temporarily "bought into" Marie's desire for me to solve her problem. I felt I had to do something to stop the daughter from making a mistake. But I knew from past experience that a clergyman can't talk a young woman in love out of her choice of a mate. Because I felt I had to solve the problem and yet couldn't do so, I felt panic. Then I became angry at being put into that situation. (In reality I had put myself into it, but I blamed Marie.) And to get out of the situation, I was going to run away from ministering to Marie.

When this particular mental tape had begun to play, my focus shifted away from Marie onto me. Because I was anxious, I reacted with panic and hostility. Now Marie had two problems: the one she came with, and me. If I had abruptly terminated our meeting, she would have left unhelped and feeling rejected. But I caught myself in time to remedy the situation.

What enabled me to catch on? First, I really did know the proper role of a pastoral listener. And the practice of reflecting upon my ministry had taught me to be alert to my feelings. My inappropriate feelings alerted me that something was wrong. Also, I suspect God may have had something to do with alerting me. I know for certain that praying the name of Jesus brought peace and clarity. This allowed me to use a structuring response that freed both of us from a misconception of ministry. Then I was able to be truly helpful to Marie.

3. *"I should be able to answer all the questions raised by a supplicant."* A memory of my succumbing to this misconception still pains me. I had been ordained only a short while when I was asked to minister to a patient dying of cancer. During my first visit she said, "Why doesn't God care about me? Why did this have to happen to me?" I didn't want her to think badly of God. I wanted her to experience God's love for her, so I tried to give a theological explanation of evil. It did not satisfy her, so I tried harder to convince her of its truth. The more I tried, the more she resisted. We ended up in a theological argument.

I was no help to this woman. She did not need a lesson in theology; she needed me to be God's ear while she told Him how angry she was about her pain. If she had felt heard by God, through my listening, perhaps she would have been ready to listen to Him through scripture, prayer and our conversation.

Conclusion

The ministry of listening is hard work and demands disciplined self-sacrifice. But it is also a rewarding ministry. We are privileged that people entrust us with so much of their lives. We see God working in the lives of others. I find that through this ministry, God reveals more of Himself to me than in any other way. I thank God for allowing me to minister as a listener. I pray that all of us who minister healing prayer may grow in our ability to listen with God's loving heart.

For Further Reading

1. *Healing Skills*, by Joseph Moore. St. Anthony Messenger Press, 1992.

2. *Emotional First-Aid Manual*, by John Steward. Para-Professional Associates, 1985.

Summary—Chapter 5

A. Four characteristics of a good pastoral care listener are:

   1. Self-sacrifice: resisting telling my own story.

   2. Respect the supplicant.

   3. Agape love: giving up the need for someone to behave, think, talk and feel according to my expectations.

   4. Serenity.

B. Listening can be enhanced by four kinds of responses:

   1. Indicating acceptance of the supplicant (not to be confused with approving of his behavior).

   2. Using reflective responses.

   3. Using focusing responses. These help the supplicant keep on track, or call her back to an important point.

   4. Using facilitating responses. These give a person permission to talk about painful topics.

C. Other helps to good ministry include:

   1. A quiet, private setting.

   2. Definite time structures (discussed in Chapter 2).

   3. Clearly agreed-upon expectations.

4. The sacred promise of confidentiality.

D. Two obstacles to good listening are anxiety and misconceptions about the task of the listener. The latter can be experienced as mental "tapes," including:

1. "I must straighten out this person."

2. "I must solve this person's problem."

3. "I should be able to answer all the questions raised by a supplicant."

For Your Reflection—Chapter 5

1. Recall an incident when someone asked you for ministry help and you consented, even though the time was inappropriate for you. After looking at the suggestions from this chapter for setting time structures and clarifying expectations, ask yourself what specific time limits would have relieved some of the pressure on you. What sort of expectations could you have clarified for this person that might have begun to meet his/her needs without placing a burden on you?

2. Recall an occasion when you, as a listener, experienced one of the obstacles to good listening: e.g., "I must solve this person's problem." How did this "mental tape" block your ability to deeply listen to the person? Where did this internal message come from? (the supplicant? someone in your childhood? your experiences as an adult? a combination of these?) What alternate "tape" can you record over this original one in order to become a better listener?

3. Read Lamentations 3:55-57, then recall an occasion when you called upon God when you were in trouble. Did you reach a point where you experienced the Lord listening to you ("being with you")? In this situation, how many of the four characteristics of a good listener did you experience in God?

6

Four Kinds of Wounds, Two Types of Remedies

❖　　❖　　❖　　❖　　❖

When I walked into Room 231 of the Burn Trauma Unit, all I could see of Reuben were his eyes and mouth. Bandages covered the rest of his body. The head nurse of the burn unit had asked me to visit this patient because he was in serious condition, unco-operative and verbally abusive to the nurses.

Reuben did not express delight at seeing me. He re-sponded to my hello by saying, "Who the hell are you?" When I told him my name and explained I was the hospital chaplain, he said, "I don't want to see no goddamn chaplain."

My heart went out to Reuben in his helpless, miserable state. I told him he looked like he was in a lot of pain.

"Pain!" said Reuben. "Are you kidding? My whole body is on fire. But that's not the worst of it. Twice a day these damn nurses soak me in a tub and scrub me down with a bristle brush. Those bitches couldn't care less how much it hurts. I always thought I was tough but it's more than *I* can take." His voice broke.

I asked Reuben how he had gotten injured. "It was so stu-pid," he said. "The foreman told me to weld a gasoline tank. 'It's safe. There's no gas in it,' he said. Like an idiot, I believed him and did what he said. It exploded in my face. Now here I am, flat on my back in this goddam hospital. I probably won't ever work again. That is, if I live." His voice broke again and he quit talking.

When I asked Reuben how his family was taking it, he said, "Damned if I know. I told 'em to keep the wife and kids out of here. If she saw me without these bandages on she would freak out. I'm ugly." He paused. "I suppose I'll be ugly the rest of my life. I don't think she can love me looking like that."

Reuben was silent a minute. Finally he said, "My wife's got enough to worry about right now. How's she gonna make the payments on the house and car? And I don't dare think about the medical bill."

At this point, a nurse interrupted us, saying it was time for Reuben's treatment. When I told him I'd see him the next day, he said, "Don't bother. There ain't nothing you can do for me. God's getting even with me."

"What for?" I asked.

"For not being a good Catholic."

"What does that mean?"

"Oh stuff like cussin' a lot," he responded, "and not going to church."

I told Reuben I'd like to visit him anyway to finish our conversation. Reluctantly he consented.

Ministering to Reuben forced me to remember the Hebrew's notion of the unity of the human person which we moderns have largely lost. We think of ourselves as composed of parts: body and soul; mind and matter. This is understandable because we are surrounded by machines that have parts we can remove, repair or replace. This leads us to think of the human person in the same way. Organ transplants, commonplace in today's medical practice, reinforce this way of thinking.

But humans are not machines; we do not consist of removable parts. I cannot accurately say, without further qualification, that my soul is more important than my body. There are no real "parts" in a human person. I am a single living unit, but such a complex unit that I need a simple way of talking about myself. I do this by identifying aspects of my personality and calling them "parts." Thus in religious circles I may speak of having a body and a soul. And I may say my soul is more important than my body. But this is just a shorthand way of communicating the truth that my relationship with God is the most important aspect of my human existence.

In this book I sometimes use this shorthand way of speaking, but in doing so I do not intend to deny the essential unity of the human person. Below, for example, I describe four types of "parts" and how they can be hurt.

Four Types of Wounds

Humans can experience pain in four areas of their existence: physical, emotional, spiritual and relational. Chapters 9 through 11 cover each of the following wounds in detail and describe how they can be ministered to. Here I cover them briefly.

1. Physical wounds

Physical wounds are damage to any part of the physical body, e.g. skin, blood, muscles, bones, organs. These can be caused by injury, by infection and disease, or by congenital defects. Physical wounds are easy to identify. For instance, a single glance at Reuben told me he was physically hurt.

2. Emotional wounds

Emotions include feelings such as joy, fear, anxiety, anger, resentment. When our emotions feel pain, they can cause us to react in distorted and destructive ways.

Deprivation and trauma are two common causes of emotional woundedness. A child raised without sufficient displays of love—not cuddled enough, not touched enough—is wounded by deprivation. Later in life, this child will find it hard to believe in his own worth. He may find it difficult to love others freely and openly.

A sexually abused child is wounded emotionally by trauma. This person, as an adult, will find it difficult to react with appropriate sexual pleasure until the wound has been healed.

Healthy emotions enable us to react to life's events in ways that allow us to achieve our purpose in life. For example, fear is a proper response to danger. It alerts us so that we can act in a way to preserve our life. Reuben's fear that he might not recover was a proper response to his life-threatening burns.

3. Spiritual wounds

Spirituality includes the mind, the will and the religious responses of the human person. Our spiritual dimension arises from our being created in God's image. God has given us a mind (the ability to know as He knows) and a will (the ability to make choices as He does).

Our spiritual dimension can be wounded. When this occurs, our wills may be affected so that we no longer choose freely. We *fall away from our likeness to God.* This can happen when our minds are given wrong or distorted information, especially about spiritual things. For example, many people have been taught to see God as a harsh, tyrannical monster - someone out to get them. This is the way Reuben felt. His misinformation prevented him from receiving God's love or giving his love to God.

Spiritual deprivation will cause spiritual woundedness. For instance, a child who is not taught the basics of religion—how to pray, who God is, who Jesus is—is spiritually deprived and will suffer the negative consequences of it as an adult. He may never come to know God and be a religious person.

Spiritual trauma is another type of spiritual woundedness. Take, for example, a young boy whose father introduces him into the world of organized crime and models that as an ideal way of life. Having been so spiritually traumatized at a young age, it is unlikely that he will ever extricate himself from a life of crime.

4. Relational wounds

Today people are keenly aware of relationships but often think of them as optional. This is false. From birth to death, we depend on others for our very existence. An infant is totally dependent on relationships for survival. If it were possible for an infant to be cared for by a machine—kept warm, fed and clean, but with no human contact—that infant would die. The adult person, while not so vulnerable, also, needs relationships with others in order to become the person God intends.

The relational dimension of our being includes relationships with the environment, with other people and with God. When these become distorted or destructive, we suffer the consequences. Reuben's way of relating to his nurses and to his wife illustrates one common source of relational wounds—immaturity. His ability to establish constructive relationships was not fully developed. He blamed the nurses for the pain he suffered during the treatment for his burns, and he verbally abused them. This was not a mature way to handle an admittedly difficult relationship. His refusal to see his wife because of his disfigurement was not a mature way of dealing with his fear of losing her love.

Relationships include the spiritual realm, that is, God, angels, and also demons. Each of these relationships can become distorted and destructive. For example, we can attempt to manipulate God to do our bidding by practicing certain rituals. We can establish destructive relationships with the world of evil spirits by seeking power through the use of occult practices. Or evil spirits can victimize us by harassment or by temptation.

The Interrelatedness of Human Hurts

Because we are a single unit with no separable parts, a wound in one dimension means the *entire* human person is wounded in some way. The hurt in one part may be so minor as to be scarcely noticeable in the other aspects of the human person. A tiny splinter in a little finger will hardly effect someone's emotional, spiritual, or relational parts. But big wounds in any dimension will impact the whole person in many ways.

Reuben's third degree burns over 50% of his body had profound repercussions in all the other aspects of his life. His emotional life suffered as he faced the possibility of death. Feelings of guilt were stirred up. His spiritual life was troubled ("God's getting even with me"). His relationships were disturbed, e.g. name-calling his foreman and the nurses who were caring for him; shutting out his wife out of fear of losing her love.

Reuben's predicament illustrates that it is not the body that is wounded, or the spirit that is wounded. It is the whole person who is hurt. Hurts sustained in one's emotional life can cause illness to the body. For example, if a hard-driving, over-achieving executive suffers a heart attack, she will need to review her set of values and the way she relates to others. Her physician may refer her for spiritual counseling as a valid treatment for her heart attack.

A man named Tom had a childhood illness that illustrates the essential unity of our being and the connectedness of the four kinds of wounds. At age 12, Tom came down with rheumatic fever, an infection of the heart muscles. He had to drop out of school and stay in bed for a year.

During his year of recovery, the illness affected more than Tom's heart. He suffered from loneliness as he lay imprisoned in his bed. He would hear his classmates go past his house after school and feel left out of their social life. He worried about his education. A teacher came to tutor him, but he feared he would fail and be humiliated by having to repeat seventh grade.

Tom's rheumatic fever also contributed to spiritual disorders. He became very anxious about his relationship to God. He felt God was punishing him for something he had done and wondered what it might be. Was it the thoughts he'd been having about sex? He was frightened. When a priest would bring him Holy Communion, he'd feel guilty but was too embarrassed to tell him his worries.

Tom's illness disrupted his relationships to family members. It made him self-centered, irritable and unpleasant to be with. He'd take out his frustrations on Bobby, his little brother. Once Bob stood by Tom's bed and teased him. Tom couldn't get out of bed, but he made a small slingshot with a rubber band and shot a steel paper clip. It hit Bob on the cheek just below the eye and caused a slight wound. When their mother found out about it, she yelled at Tom for doing something so dangerous. He cried and felt rejected by her. In the aftermath of this event, he had a physical setback from which it took him weeks to recover.

Tom told me this story as an adult. He ended it saying, "It wasn't my heart that was sick. It was *me* that was sick, and I was sick *all over*."

Two Types of Remedies

Ministers of religious healing need to become aware of all of the remedies God has given us for the healing of wounds. These remedies fall into two basic categories: natural and supernatural.

Natural remedies are part of God's general plan of creation and are available to all human beings. God has given them to us precisely because we are his creatures. Natural remedies include:

- medical treatment,
- psychiatric care,
- marriage and family counseling,
- knowledge of nutrition and exercise,
- listening and instruction.

Supernatural remedies arise from an awareness that we are more than creatures of God. Through faith in Christ and baptism, we are God's children. God has adopted us into his family, and we share in his divine nature (2 Peter 1:4). This is the meaning of supernatural. We are living a life beyond our natural human powers.[1]

God, as a loving Father, has given us the means of healing that are in accord with our new nature. These are the supernatural ways of healing. They include remedies that can be administered by any Christian—e.g. prayer, scripture, sacramentals—and those that are reserved to ordained ministers—e.g. certain blessings, sacraments.

---

1. I explore this difficult concept further in Chapter 3 of *Healing as a Parish Ministry* (by Thomas and Alkire; published in 1992 by Ave Maria Press, Notre Dame)

Combined Remedies

Each one of the four kinds of human hurts can be healed by either natural or supernatural remedies or by a combination of both. We use these remedies in trust that God will care for our every need.

For instance, Reuben's primary hurt was physical—third-degree burns. For this he was receiving intensive medical treatment: medicines and daily removal of dead tissue to promote new growth. His body responded well and started to heal quickly. Later, doctors did skin grafts and cosmetic surgery. As a result, Reuben suffered no permanent scars on his face and only minor ones on his arms and body.

A psychiatric social worker helped Reuben deal with his fears that his disfigurement would repulse his wife and children. Finally, he allowed them to visit him.

With the family present, I administered the sacraments of Anointing of the Sick and Holy Communion. This celebration did much to heal family relationships as well as Reuben's body. Their visible signs of love allayed his fears that his disfigured body repulsed them. After several visits, I explained inner healing, and Reuben allowed me to pray for emotional healing of the fear and anxiety resulting from the accident. This, along with psychiatric counseling, helped him became more hopeful about his situation.

The spiritual dimension of Reuben's illness was the most difficult to heal. After many meetings, he trusted me enough to tell me he thought God was a harsh and punitive person. I encouraged him to talk more about this, and when he seemed ready to hear a different point of view, I read him the story of the Father and the Prodigal Son. Reuben broke into sobs during my reading and told me his own father had been physically abusive, often beating him for small infractions of household rules. Reuben spoke vehemently of how he still hated his father. I prayed a number of times with him for inner healing of these terrible experiences. He finally experienced healing of his memories and was able to forgive his deceased father. He made use of the Sacrament of Reconciliation and experienced forgiveness and peace. After this, his negative attitudes towards God changed quickly, and he became eager to read the Bible.

Reuben was discharged from the hospital but continued treatment as an outpatient. I did not see him for many months. One day I heard a knock on my office door and looked up to see Reuben standing in the doorway. He had a big grin on his face.

"Hi, Father!" he said. "I came by to tell you my treatments are finished. I'm back on the job and doing okay. My face came out pretty good, didn't it? Hardly any marks at all. I just want to say thanks for everything."

An example of combined remedies for spiritual healing

When I reached the end of the cafeteria line and looked around the dining room of the retreat house for a place to sit, I noticed a man sitting alone by the window. His dignity and bearing made me want to know him better, so I asked if I could join him. He smiled, motioned to a chair, and said his name was Mark.

I asked Mark how the retreat was going for him. He leaned back in his chair, looked out at the grounds of the retreat house and said he could hardly believe he was in a place like this. Two years ago, he had been traveling with a whole different crowd and couldn't have imagined this way of life existed. He told me that in his whole life, he had never even heard about God except as a "cuss word or a joke."

Intrigued, I asked Mark if he would be willing to share his story with me. He told me that when he was twenty-two, he joined a motorcycle gang widely known for its lawlessness. He had fully participated in its violent way of life. Two years later he had a serious motorcycle accident. While recovering in a Catholic hospital, the chaplain visited him.

Mark was favorably impressed by the chaplains' friendliness and by the religious sisters who nursed him. Their behavior made him curious about the Catholic religion. He started asking the chaplain religious questions. Before he left the hospital, he said he wanted to learn more about the Catholic faith. So the chaplain arranged for him to have a course of instructions.

Through this instruction he experienced a conversion, and at the end of the course he asked to be baptized in the Catholic church.

At one point in our conversation, I asked Mark why he'd joined the motorcycle gang. He answered that it was "simply because I didn't have anything else to believe in or anything else better to do. I had to do something to fill that terrible emptiness." When he discovered in the Inquiry Class that there was a God who loved him enough to send His own son to find him, he was dumfounded. Mark said it was "too good to be true." It took a long time for him to believe this fact. But once he could believe, he wanted nothing else but to follow Jesus' way of life.

The ministry of spiritual healing demands great sensitivity to the condition of the recipient, plus a thorough command of the many means of healing at the disposal of the minister. Mark told me that twice earlier he had been approached by a Christian filled with evangelistic zeal who warned him, "You will die in your sins and go to everlasting damnation unless you repent and accept Jesus as your savior!" Mark told me, "This meant nothing to me. I merely dismissed it as the ravings of a religious nut."

Both the hospital chaplain and the nursing sisters showed sensitivity to Mark's spiritual condition. In his first visits, the chaplain did not talk about spirituality until Mark indicated an openness to discussing this. Considering the stage he was at, the religious sisters' loving care of him contributed more to healing his spiritual wounds than would any talk about the state of his soul.

The beginning of Mark's spiritual healing, then, started with the natural means of ordinary human friendliness and loving nursing care. This healing continued through the course of instruction he took. Now supernatural means of healing entered into the picture. The Word of God, communicated sensitively and in a planned sequence, changed Mark. The course of instruction filled his mind with correct knowledge of God and gave his will the ability to make new choices. He decided to respond to God's Word and to change his way of life. He asked for Baptism and received the Sacraments of Confirmation and the Eucharist.

After Mark's conversion, he found he still had many un-christian attitudes left from his earlier way of life. Here the ministry of healing prayer was used. He asked members of a prayer group to pray for the healing of these attitudes. He also found the Sacrament of Reconciliation helpful in strengthening his will to do the right things.

When I met him, Mark was attending a retreat because his confessor had told him retreats are a powerful aid in healing spiritual woundedness. Mark reported that the Eucharist was removing the terrible emptiness he had felt from his teen years. His healing was the most thoroughgoing spiritual healing I have encountered, and I learned much from him.

An example of combined remedies for healing relationships

Two teammates and I had just finished a workshop at a religious conference when a woman approached us. Smiling, she told us her name was Irene and wanted us to know how much we had done for her and her family. "You have changed our lives," she said.

At a similar conference two years earlier, Irene had heard our presentation, *The Power of Affirmation as a Way of Life*. During that presentation she had had to admit to herself that she had come to the conference to get away from Robbie, her eleven-year-old son. He and Irene had been locked in constant conflict since he was an infant, and it was destroying the entire family.

Listening to our presentation, Irene realized she had never affirmed Robbie in his entire life. All she had done was put him down. In the middle of our presentation, Irene had started crying. "I asked Jesus to forgive me," she told us later, "and promised him I would become an affirming person. I started to make a list of things I could affirm in Robbie." She didn't even wait until she got home to start the affirming process. Instead, she called Robbie on the phone and told him she loved him and mentioned one of his special qualities. He was shocked, but after a while he said, "I love you, too, Mom."

Irene told us that when she returned home, she started a program of affirming Robbie and the other family members. By the end of the second year, the family was so completely changed that Irene's husband decided to come to the conference to see for himself what had transformed the family.

Here, an ordinary lecture and the very human practice of affirmation started the process of healing this family's wounded relationships. But Irene wisely used every means of healing at her disposal. She told us she'd sought prayer to heal her part in the conflict. She had not wanted another child, and when she became pregnant with Robbie, she had turned her resentment upon him.

Irene made frequent use of the Sacrament of Reconciliation to take away the effects of the sin of resentment and anger that had accumulated over the years. She prayed each day that the Lord would help her call upon the grace of the Sacrament of Matrimony. She found the grace of the Sacrament was a powerful help to her; it helped her make Christ's love real to the entire family.

Conclusion

We humans are marvelously complex creations of God. We are meant to share in God's joy, but we are vulnerable. So many bad things happen to us. God wants us well and so has given us, through Christ, many remedies to heal our ills. Healing is a ministry so dear to the heart of Jesus that he commissions us to continue his healing presence in the world. He wants us to learn by prayer, study, and experience how better to make his healing presence felt by all those in need.

For Further Reading

1. *Handbook for Ministers of Care,* by Marily Kofler and Kevin O'Rourke. Liturgy Training Publications, 1987.
2. *Healing,* by Francis MacNutt. Ave Maria Press, 1974.

Summary—Chapter 6

A. This chapter describes four kinds of wounds:

1. *Physical*: includes any physical part of the human body

2. *Emotional*: painful feelings that can be caused by deprivation or trauma

3. *Spiritual*: a falling away from the likeness of God. This may be caused by spiritual deprivation or spiritual trauma, including being given wrong or distorted information about spiritual matters.

4. *Relational*: wounds from distorted or destructive relationships. This can impact relationships with God, the Body of Christ, the deceased, angels and the physical environment.

B. Because a person is a single unit with no separable parts, a wound in one dimension means the entire person is wounded in some way.

C. God uses both natural and supernatural means to heal the four kinds of wounds.

1. *Natural remedies* include medicine, counseling, listening and instructing.

2. *Supernatural remedies* include those that may be administered by any Christian (e.g., prayer, Scripture, sacramentals) and those whose administration is reserved to ordained ministers (e.g., certain blessings, sacraments). Ministers of religious healing use supernatural remedies as adopted children of God who share in his divine nature.

For Your Reflection—Chapter 6

1. This chapter asserts that because a person is a single unit with no separable parts, a wound in one dimension means the entire person is wounded in some way. Recall a time when you were suffering physically. How did it impact you emotionally? spiritually? in your relationships with others? Were you aware of this broader impact at the time, or only upon reflection?

2. Recall a time when you, or someone you know, had a serious physical illness. What remedies (natural and/or supernatural) were used to bring about physical healing? Was anything done to bring about healing of the emotional, spiritual and/or relational wounds arising from this illness? If yes, what remedies were used? If no, what might have been helpful?

3. Read Mt 9:1-8. Before Jesus healed the paralyzed man, he asked the teachers of the Law, "Which is easier to say, 'Your sins are forgiven,' or to say 'Get up and walk'?" In other words, which is easier—spiritual healing or physical healing? Which type of healing do *you* think is easier? When you are in need of spiritual or physical healing, which is easier for you to experience through all the routes available to you (including medicine and counseling)?

7

Healing Physical Hurts

❖   ❖   ❖   ❖   ❖

Father Anthony was only 40 when he died. He and I had been members of the same religious order and of the same prayer group. Now I was in the prior's office being asked if I wanted to preach the homily at Fr. Anthony's funeral Mass. "Fr. Anthony told me he wanted you to do it," he said. "How do you feel about that?"

I knew what the Prior was thinking. Fr. Anthony had died after a six-month struggle with cancer, and I had ministered prayer for healing to him during that time. Now the Prior was wondering if I thought he was asking me to bury one of my "failures."

I appreciated the Prior's sensitivity to my situation, but did not consider Fr. Anthony to be one of my failures. Instead, I told the prior that I *wanted* to preach the homily because I felt it would complete my ministry to Fr. Anthony.

Two months earlier I could not have said that. Then I *was* feeling like a failure. But my recent ministry to Tony had radically changed my understanding of healing prayer.

The prayer group that Tony and I belonged to had only recently learned about prayer for healing and had started the practice of praying with supplicants at the end of the general prayer meeting. So when Fr. Anthony received his medical diagnosis, he asked us to pray with him for healing. Shocked by the news, for the first few weeks we prayed over him fervently at every opportunity. During these times of prayer, several people prophesied that he would be healed. The community—rather frantically, I thought—exhorted Fr. Anthony to have expectant faith that he would be healed.

This was in the early days of the healing ministry and we were inexperienced. When dramatic and instantaneous healing did not occur, we became confused. Our prayers became chaotic and undisciplined. Finally, two leaders and I held a meeting with Fr. Anthony and discussed why healing was not happening. We decided something else needed to happen first. We had heard of "healing of memories" and decided we should pray for that first. We also had heard that unforgiveness blocks healing, so we would help Fr. Anthony look for areas of unforgiveness. We decided that only the three of us would pray with him on a regular basis. Fr. Anthony agreed with this plan.

The new approach proved fruitful. Fr. Anthony surfaced many painful memories that were healed. He also looked openly at a seriously wounded relationship with an older brother. They had not spoken since the death of their father, at which time they had quarreled over disposing of the family home.

But in spite of all this ministry, Fr. Anthony's physical condition worsened. I told the team I thought we needed to help him face the possibility of death. They reluctantly agreed but asked me to speak with him privately first.

Fr. Anthony was now confined to bed most of the time. I visited him and gingerly asked him if he'd considered that he might not be healed. He said, yes, the doctor had talked openly about death as a real possibility, but he was trying not to dwell on it. "I've not wanted to think negative thoughts."

I suggested to Fr. Anthony that we take a two track approach: complete healing as one possibility, and death as another. I proposed that we pursue both. Tony said it would be a relief to be able to talk openly about death; it had been hard to avoid those thoughts.

Looking at the prospect of death enabled Fr. Anthony to make several decisions. First, he decided he wanted reconciliation with his older brother. So he phoned him and asked him to come visit. Second, he felt sad that death would mean he could not continue to help his widowed sister raise her three small children. He felt close to her and had been an active father-figure to her children. So he decided to make a series of audio tapes that the children could listen to when they were older. He wanted them to know about himself and about their family history. Finally, Fr. Anthony was chairman of the theology department in the seminary and wanted to get the records in good order so that someone else could take over in the event of his death.

During the time Fr. Anthony was preparing for the possibility of death, we continued to pray for healing. One day, however, he said, "Please don't pray for physical healing anymore. It's too hypocritical. I can no longer believe that God is going to heal me." I sensed the bitterness in his voice and mentioned it. He said, "Yes, I'm bitter. Others have received healing through my prayer; why doesn't Jesus heal me? He's abandoned me to my pain." At this, he started to cry and I cried with him. He had voiced a question that had troubled all of us, a question we had tried to ignore.

This was a time of spiritual struggle for all of us. Why were our prayers for healing not being heard? At our next prayer time, the team discussed this openly with Fr. Anthony. Although several possibilities occurred to us, none of them rang true. I suggested we spend the entire session praying about our lack of success. Fr. Anthony agreed, but without enthusiasm.

We read several scripture verses in which God promised his continued presence, and then prayed with them in mind. I summed up the prayer time with a prayer: "Father, your son Anthony is sick. While Jesus walked this earth, he healed all who came to him. We have followed his command to lay hands upon the sick and heal them. Why is Anthony not healed? Father, you seem so silent, so far away. Please make your loving presence known to Anthony and to us." Our prayer ended with a profound sense of God's silence.

The next day Fr. Anthony was a changed person. He was eager to tell us what had happened. During the night when he was in considerable pain he cried out with bitterness to God, accusing him of not caring that he hurt. "Why don't you *do* something for me?" he cried.

Suddenly, Fr. Anthony had had an image of himself as a small child when he had been critically ill with a kidney disease. In the mental picture he was in the hospital and his dad was standing by the bed. A concerned physician and a nurse were also there. His dad was sobbing with grief. Then, in the image, his human father was replaced by God as Father who was also sobbing with grief, feeling very helpless in the face of Fr. Anthony's suffering. At that moment Fr. Anthony *felt* God's compassion for him, and *knew* that God had done everything He possibly could for him, including sending his Son Jesus to heal him. Tony was so graphic in his description that we could feel what he felt. Although he did not have an intellectual answer to the question of why he was not being healed, he now "knew" that God cared.

Our ministry to Fr. Anthony was a turning point in my understanding of the ministry of religious healing. It forced me to give up the simplistic understanding of healing that says, "You just pray with faith and God heals." It made me undertake the effort, which still continues, to penetrate the divine mystery involved in healing. I've discovered that, as with all divine mysteries, the more one learns about healing, the deeper the mystery becomes.

After his experience of God's compassion, Fr. Anthony wanted to pray more but was hindered by the stupefying effects of his pain medication. He discussed with the physician the feasibility of discontinuing the pain medication. The doctor told him that the withdrawal symptoms would be severe, and without medication the pain would be unbearable. Fr. Anthony asked us to pray specifically that he could do without this medication. We did so, and Fr. Anthony was able to do without pain medicine completely with no withdrawal symptoms and very little pain. After this he spent most of his time in prayer and was almost constantly in God's presence. He told us, "This is the best time I have ever had with God."

Toward the end, Fr. Anthony asked me if I would preach at his funeral Mass. He said he knew many members of the prayer group would be hurt and confused because in spite of our ministry and of the prophecies that he would be healed, he had died.

He asked that in my preaching I make clear that although a battle had been lost, a victory had been won. Jesus had not been defeated, he had won the victory for which he died and rose.

Health and Healing

The most basic concept in the mystery of physical healing is the religious meaning of the word "health." Physicians generally use health to indicate a lack of disease of the human organism. When disease afflicts the human organism, doctors use the word "healing" to mean any intervention by physical, chemical or surgical methods to overcome that disease.

But the *religious* meaning of health is quite different: it means wholeness—the very wholeness of God. Jesus proclaimed this message: the human person, wounded by sin, is being called into God's own wholeness. And the *religious* meaning of "healing" is God's activity, in Christ, bringing us into that wholeness.[1]

The religious meaning of healing is the ongoing process of transformation of the person into a new reality. This transformation is the work of Christ, who has bestowed on us the gift of sharing in the Father's divine nature (2 Pt 1:4). St. Paul described this transformation this way: "When anyone is joined to Christ he is a new being: the old is gone, the new has come." (TEV, 2 Cor 5:17)

St. John expressed the same reality using the idea of new birth: "I am telling you the truth: no one can see the Kingdom of God unless he is born again." (TEV, Jn 3:3), and

"Some, however, did receive him and believed in him; so he gave them the right to become God's children; . . . God himself was their Father." (TEV, Jn 1:12-13)

In the ongoing process of transformation, physical healing is a part—but only a part—of God's mending of the human person. God transforms her into the new creation she is intended to be. The total transformation also includes mending the emo-

---

1. I deal in greater detail with the question of health and healing in Chapter 3 of *Healing as a Parish Ministry* (by Thomas and Alkire; Notre Dame: Ave Maria Press, 1992).

tional, spiritual and relational aspects of the person. *From a religious perspective, physical health is not an end in itself apart from the transformation of the total person.* For the Christian, wellness is a state of being that enables her to travel on her spiritual journey towards God's own wholeness.

These truths must be kept in mind when talking about praying for physical healing. The healing team's task is to proclaim, to inaugurate and to portray God's call to become a new creation. Success is not be measured solely by overcoming disease. That's *part* of, but not the totality of, success. If a team's ministry enables their supplicant, in any degree, to move closer to God's wholeness, to that degree their ministry has been successful. Our ministry to Fr. Anthony succeeded to the extent that it contributed to his transformation. Through our ministry, he became more of a son of God than he would have been without it.

It is also true that Fr. Anthony's medical treatment succeeded to the extent that it contributed to his ability to continue on his spiritual journey. From a purely medical understanding of health and healing, both the physician's treatment and our prayer for physical healing would have been called failures. But from a religious understanding of these terms, they were successful.

But even from a religious understanding of health and healing, we did not succeed entirely in our ministry to Fr. Anthony. He did not recover from his physical illness as ideally he should have. To that degree, our ministry failed. Both team and supplicant should expect healing to be part of God's loving response to a supplicant's need. But how and when this will come about is another question.[2]

How Religious Healing Works

The beginning of our ministry to Fr. Anthony was flawed in two ways: 1) Our approach was super-spiritualistic in that the focus of our attention was on dramatic results. 2) We lacked a

2. Chapter 6 of *Healing as a Parish Ministry* (op. cit.) goes into greater detail regarding criteria for success or failure in healing ministry.

sufficient appreciation of the organic unity of the human person. We acted as if we could separate Fr. Anthony's physical illness from all the other aspects of his humanity. Fr. Anthony's request for physical healing plunged him and us into his total spiritual journey. Unexpectedly we became involved in someone's journey of transformation.

Both these errors narrowed our vision and blinded us from seeing God's presence. We thought our ministry was not producing results. Only out of apparent failure could we give up a super-spiritualistic approach. Failure opened our minds sufficiently to start praying for healing in Fr. Anthony's emotional, spiritual and relational dimensions, as well as in the physical. Understanding the religious meaning of health and healing would have spared all of us much anguish and confusion. But we had not yet learned this truth. We learned it by reflecting upon our "failed" ministry.

Fr. Anthony's input was crucial to our understanding of what God was doing. Both he and I had been trained in theology. This helped. One day, after he had passed his spiritual crisis, I asked him if the team had done anything especially helpful. He said, "That time you wept with me when I complained to God why he hadn't healed me, why he had abandoned me." He told me my weeping allowed him to experience God's compassion. At that moment, he felt I was God-for-him. If I had given up on him, he thought he might never have experienced God's compassion for him.

I asked Fr. Anthony how we might grasp this theologically. As we discussed our ministry, we saw that incarnational theology is critical to the understanding the ministry of religious healing. Super-spiritualism overvalues God's part in healing and undervalues the minister's part. In our ministry we initially had used slogans such as "It is God who heals, we only pray." But an incarnational view of healing would say that any healing that occurs comes totally from God as *source* and *cause* of healing, and totally from the team as *instruments* God uses to transmit his healing power.

Instruments of God's Healing Power

Jesus is Lord of every part of the universe. Col 1:16-17 (TEV) tells us "God created the whole universe through him and for him, . . . and in union with him all things have their proper place." Thus Jesus is able to use *all* creation to achieve his purposes, including healing. He uses antibiotics, chemotherapy, psychological counseling, the natural healing forces in the human body, and the ministry of prayer to heal a sick person. God works as powerfully in the administration of an antibiotic as he does in the ministry of religious healing. This means we must be humble about our ministry. We must respect medical science as part of God's loving care of his children.

Incarnational theology tells us, then, that in the ministry of religious healing God chooses to use us as instruments. Using music to illustrate this point, Beethoven composed music in his mind. He could sit in the silence of his deafness and "hear" his music, note by note. But if he had come out onto the stage of a concert hall and just "thought" his music with no orchestra playing it, the world would never have received his gift of music. When Beethoven wrote out the score of the music he had mentally composed and gave it to an orchestra to perform, the music came totally from Beethoven as its creator. Yet it also came totally from the musical instruments—empowered by human players—producing the sounds Beethoven intended.

Just as Beethoven used orchestral instruments to give his gift of music to the world, so God uses us as *living* instruments to give his gift of wholeness to all of creation. However, humans differ from musical instruments. We are endowed with intelligence and free will. When God uses us as instruments, He respects our nature as he created it. He does not treat us as lifeless puppets. Even though we are instruments in God's hands, we must act in fully human ways. We use our intelligence, which we must develop by study and reflection upon our ministry. In ministry we make choices; we must learn to make loving choices by living disciplined Christian lives. Because God respects our human nature, we can temporarily frustrate God's work by not being well-prepared, living instruments, even as a piano can frustrate a musician by being out of tune.

So although healing comes totally from God, unless we do our part, ordinarily healing will not happen. God could heal directly without any ministry on our part. But he has chosen to use us because we are members of Christ's Body. All that God does is now done through Christ.

Religious Healing is a Process

A friend's three-year-old son, Angelo, had a rash on his body. My friend decided it needed a physician's attention, so she prepared Angelo for an appointment by explaining how the doctor would make it well. The physician examined the rash, made a mental diagnosis, wrote a prescription with directions for its use, and gave it to the mother. He then told Angelo he could put his clothes back on and indicated that the visit was over.

As the doctor started to leave the room, Angelo looked down at the rash and called out, "Doctor, the bumps are still there!" The doctor came back into the room and explained that his mother would have to buy some medicine and rub it on his "bumps" three times a day for three days, and then they would gradually go away. This satisfied Angelo. Until it was explained, he had been thinking of healing in a non-process way.

Physical healing is a process that prayer can affect in several ways:

- It may bring healing without the use of medicine or surgery.
- It may speed up the process of healing, even to the point where it appears to be instantaneous.
- It may lessen the side effects of a medication, such as the nausea that results from chemotherapy treatment of cancer.
- It may strengthen the effects of a medication or treatment beyond what would normally be expected.

In Fr. Anthony's case, prayer enabled him to withdraw from an addictive pain medication without experiencing normal withdrawal symptoms. It also lessened his pain so that he did not need pain medication. His lessening of pain was permanent; sometimes it is only temporary.

One caution about praying for the cessation of pain: Pain is a signal that something is wrong and needs attention. It is not good to turn off that signal before it receives proper attention. If someone comes to us with severe chest pains and does not know whether he is experiencing a heart attack or indigestion, it would be unwise to pray for a cessation of pain until he has visited a physician and received a diagnosis. On other hand, it was appropriate for us to pray for cessation of pain for Fr. Anthony, who had been diagnosed and was under medical care.

The Healing of Fr. Anthony

For my homily at Fr. Anthony's funeral, I used a Scripture text from the book of Wisdom:

> In the eyes of the unwise, they did appear to die, their going looked like a disaster, their leaving us, like an annihilation; but they are in peace. (JB, Wis. 3:2-3)

I opened the homily by saying if ever a death looked like a disaster, Fr Anthony's did. He did not want to die. He struggled against death with all his might. He was young; he had much to give; he had ministry to do; family, community, friends to love. His illness was long and painful. He died hollow-eyed and gaunt. "Where is the victory?" I asked.

My opening statement highlighted the fact that our ministry was not entirely successful. But then I went on to say that through the ministry of religious healing, Fr. Anthony did receive healing in all four dimensions of his being. Although his physical healing was restricted to freedom from pain and medication, it was significant. It freed him to grow in all the other areas of his life, especially in his relationship with God.

In the emotional dimension, the reconstruction of childhood experiences freed Fr. Anthony from patterns of response to life situations that had hindered his spiritual journey. This inner healing enabled him to overcome his fear of dying. It prevented the apathy that so often dominates the seriously ill. His refusal to be mastered by pain, fear and discouragement was a significant victory.

Fr. Anthony received healing of his spiritual wounds. He was healed of his distorted notion of God as distant and uncaring and came to see Him as a caring, compassionate Parent. This opened the way for him to make new choices. He chose not to become a *victim* of cancer or of death. He refused to become depersonalized by his illness; instead he became more of a person. He came to know who he was as a child of God, and the meaning of his life. His visitors were surprised at the energy they felt flowing from him. One frequent visitor said, "I always left Tony's room feeling better than when I entered. He gave me a lot more than I gave him."

I think the greatest healing was in Fr. Anthony's relationships. He resisted the temptation to become alienated from God. He did not allow feelings of despair to destroy his friendship with God. He struggled with them and came to know God more intimately.

Fr. Anthony refused to become hidden away with his illness. He chose to live his last few months with his religious community rather than in the hospital. He maintained his interest in community affairs, his family, and friends. With his refusal to be *just* a dying patient, he understood that the Lord had work for him to do even while he was sick, and he did that work. He became reconciled with his brother and provided for a continuing relationship with his sister's children. For all of us, his friends, he gave a Christian witness. He showed us how to triumph over death. He pioneered the way. Each of us, his friends, now knows what it means to be a traveler on the road to God's own wholeness.

For Further Reading

1. *The Call to Wholeness: Health as a Spiritual Journey,* by Kenneth L. Bakken. Crossroad Publishers, 1985.

Summary—Chapter 7

A. The religious meaning of health and healing differs from the medical community's use of them.

   1. *Health*: In medicine it is the absence of disease. Its religious meaning, though, is the wholeness of God.

   2. *Healing*: Medically it is any intervention by physical, chemical or surgical methods to overcome a disease. Religiously, healing is the ongoing process of transformation of a person into a new reality. This transformation is the work of Christ, who has bestowed on us the gift of sharing in the divine nature.

B. Physical healing is only one part of God's mending of the human person. Total transformation includes emotional, spiritual and relational healing. To the degree a prayer team enables a supplicant to travel better on his journey towards God's wholeness, ministry is a success.

C. God uses us—and all of creation—to give His gift of wholeness to hurting people. He uses our intelligence, which we must develop. Healing comes totally from God, but unless we do our part, ordinarily healing will not occur.

D. Physical healing is a process which prayer can affect:

   1. It may bring healing without medicine or surgery.

   2. It may speed up the process of healing, even to the point where it appears to be instantaneous.

   3. It may lessen the side effects of a medication.

   4. It may strengthen the effects of a medication or treatment beyond what would normally be expected.

For Your Reflection—Chapter 7

1. Reflect on a time when you, like Father Anthony, felt bitter towards God while in the midst of your own or someone else's suffering. Did you end up experiencing God's compassion in that situation? If yes, relive that experience in the light of what you've learned here. If you didn't experience God's compassion, how did you resolve your feelings of anger/bitterness?

2. Even though Father Anthony died, his prayer team claimed their ministry was a success because he moved closer to God's wholeness, spiritually and emotionally. Do you agree with their evaluation? Why or why not?

3. Incompetent and spiritually immature ministers can wreck God's plan to heal someone, just as poor musicians can ruin Beethoven's *5th Symphony*. Recall a time when you experienced a failure of ministry, either as a supplicant or as a minister. In what specific ways do you think God's plan was blocked by human actions (or inactions)? Envision how that situation might have been handled in a more competent, spiritually mature way.

4. Read 2 Peter 1:3-4, then reflect on its statement that Christians "share the divine nature." How much of a struggle is it for you to accept that your redemption includes such a radical transformation? Compare this passage to Paul's statement in 2 Cor 5:17, where he says, "When anyone is joined to Christ he is a new being." Are you willing to accept this amazing invitation?

8

Healing Emotional Ills

❖   ❖   ❖   ❖   ❖

One summer day when I was five years old, my parents and I went for a drive in the country. We stopped at a park for a picnic lunch and, while my mother was setting out the food, my father walked down the street to buy something from a nearby store. I was exploring the park some distance from my mother. Suddenly a pack of dogs attacked me! With salvia drooling from gaping mouths, they knocked me down and were about to devour me. I screamed with terror, and my mother rescued me. She tried to calm me, but I would not be comforted because the dogs continued to surround me, barking, jumping, and trying to get me.

I remember how utterly terrified I was of these animals. My father, hearing my screams, ran back from the store, sized up the situation, took me in his arms and carried me into the car, where he shut the door against these beasts. He asked me to tell him what had happened. Still sobbing, I told him the story of my near destruction.

When I was done, he reminded me of something that had happened to me a few months earlier. Our neighbor, Mr. Foraker, had a dog named Queenie. One day he said he wanted to show me something. He took me into his garage and there was Queenie with six newborn puppies. I wanted to pick them up, but Mr. Foraker said they were too little. In a few weeks I could play with them. Every day I asked Mr. Foraker if the puppies were big enough yet. Finally one day he said they were, and he brought all six of them out into the yard. I lay down and they climbed all over me, licking my face and biting my fingers and toes. I laughed and rolled over and over, and they kept licking and biting and jumping all over me.

My father got me into remembering what fun I'd had with the puppies and how I played with them every day until they got big. After they were given away, I was sad; I missed them! Then my father said, "The dogs that frightened you were puppies like Queenie's, only bigger. They wanted to play with you; they wanted to roll on the ground with you and to lick your face and bite your toes. But they were too big and you were too little."

I knew my father was the smartest man in the whole world, but surely he was wrong this time. Those dogs didn't want to play; they wanted to kill me! I was convinced of that.

Reading my looks, my father suggested we play a pretend game: "Pretend those dogs are here again; they've knocked you down and are standing over you. Only this time, I'm with you. I will protect you. Now pretend you are *very* big. Reach out and pet one of the dogs; now scratch its stomach. Now pull its tail, but don't hurt it, and watch it try to bite your hand. Are you pretending?"

"Yes, Daddy," I answered in a quivering voice.

My father asked me what was happening in my pretend time. I told him that the dog I was petting didn't look as big as it did before and that it was licking my hand. My father then said I could quit pretending.

After talking about pretend games for a few minutes, my father said something that struck fear in my five-year-old heart: "Let's go find the dogs and play with them for real. Only this time I will be with you to protect you." Timidly I went along with him. We found the dogs and I tried to be brave, but I was scared. My father didn't let them knock me over this time; he held me as I gingerly patted one of the dogs while he kept the others away. I didn't enjoy it very much, but it did seem like it might be fun if the dog was smaller and if there was only one of them. I told him this, and the next day he brought home a tiny puppy to be my very own dog. I named her Spot. She was my friend for many years.

The Reconstruction of Experience

My father had done for me what Robert L. Wise in his book, *Healing of the Past,* calls "the reconstruction of experience."[1] He prefers this term to the more familiar ones: "Healing of the Memories" and "Inner Healing." Wise says that our emotional ills can be understood in this way:

- An experience that wounded me in the past, especially in early childhood, still affects my behavior just as it did at the time it happened, even though I now "know better."

- Even though I may have forgotten the event with my conscious mind, it still resides in my unconscious memory and still influences my behavior. The constant and irrational repetition of past behavior is the emotional wound that needs healing.

- Until it is healed, I am not free to respond as I would like and know I should. I am in bondage to the earlier wounding experience.

- The wound can be healed by bringing it into conscious memory and reliving it in the light of Christ's healing presence so that the original event is reconstructed. This means *it will be perceived differently, have a different meaning for me and have a different outcome.*

Although Wise calls this an "explanation," he says clearly it remains a mystery because it is the work of the Holy Spirit making Jesus present to a supplicant and, in so doing, healing his emotional wounds. The explanation helps in understanding how healing prayer works, but ultimately it remains in the realm of faith. However, this partial understanding takes away the "spookiness" that many people feel when they first hear of this ministry, and it makes ministers more effective in ministering healing to emotional hurts.

If my father had not healed my experience of being "attacked by a pack of dogs," I would have grown up with an unrea-

---

1. Robert L. Wise, *Healing of the Past: Recovering Emotional and Mental Wholeness.* Oklahoma City: Presbyterian and Reformed Ministries International, 1984.

sonable and exaggerated fear of dogs—even of harmless, playful puppies.

Compare what my father did for me with the prayer team's ministry to Larry in Chapter 3: Although my father did not see his actions as ministry, and although he did not invoke the presence of Jesus or make use of prayer, it was healing of an emotional hurt through the use of natural means. It had many similarities to the ministry of healing emotional hurts.

In Chapter 3, Larry was handicapped by feelings that he could never measure up to anyone's expectations of him. His feelings grew out of childhood experiences of being ridiculed by his father for not measuring up. These experience were capsulized in the memory of bringing home a report card with a failing grade and being made to wear a dunce cap at the dinner table while everyone called him the "family dummy."

Even before Larry's prayer team asked him to relive this memory in his imagination, Larry experienced God affirming his gifts and approving of him as a well loved son. This was a deeply moving experience for him. It set the stage for the next phase of healing.

The team instructed Larry to remember the humiliating scene at the dinner table and then invite Jesus into the setting. Larry reported that with Jesus present in the remembered scene, the entire event took a different turn than it had in the original occurrence. In the reconstructed event, Jesus came to the table, removed the dunce cap from Larry and comforted him as he was crying. Jesus talked to him about his troubles with English Composition and then asked one of Larry's older sisters to help him with his homework. Jesus then talked to Larry's father about his own childhood hurts that made him act so cruel to his son. The father received healing in this scene, and Larry was able to understand and forgive his father. Jesus reminded the entire family that they all were part of God's family; as they grasped this, they were able to love and support one another. In the reenacted scene, the family experienced profound reconciliation.

This is only a summary of a powerful experience that took several sessions. Note the similarities of what my father did for me and what the team did in ministry with Larry. In getting me to tell him what had happened, my father helped me relive my wounding experience with the dogs.

Prayer often enables someone to recall what is at the root of his troubling symptoms. In the context of prayer, the team helps the supplicant relive the wounding experience by asking him to remember it as vividly and as graphically as possible. If the wound has been the result of repeated events, such as a parent constantly belittling a child as Larry's dad did, it is well to get the supplicant to sum up the problem in a single specific event, such as Larry's remembering his father making him wear a dunce cap at the dinner table.

The next step in the reconstruction of the wounding event is to develop a new understanding of the event and some new options of how to respond to the event. My father's story of my playing with Queenie's puppies stirred my imagination, and I could vicariously live it out as he told it. This gave me a new understanding of dogs and their behavior, and a new way of relating to them. He could have simply told me that the dogs were only playful puppies, but he was wise enough to know that would not do the job. My perceptions had to be changed, but just *telling* me was not enough to change my perceptions.

Many times in ministry we are tempted to "explain" things to a supplicant—to tell him he has not understood a situation correctly. Sometimes new knowledge is helpful (e.g. in the ministry of instruction—Chapter 15). But if we want to change a supplicant's perception of an experience that is influencing his behavior, it won't work to merely inform him that his perception is incorrect.

The key to changing behavior is to change the images that motivate one to act. In ordinary language we say we are "thinking about" doing something. This is shorthand for a complex mental process that includes the use of images, although we are seldom aware of the images. To do the simplest thing—e.g. sitting down—I first must have an image in my mind of this act—of the chair I will sit on, of the various bodily movements involved in sitting down. When charm schools teach young women how to walk gracefully, they give them a new set of images through watching other students and then practicing what they have seen.[2]

My father's story about Queenie started the process of changing my experience. He gave me another set of images: Dogs knock you down and lick your face and bite your toes for reasons other than a desire to eat you. I began to see this as a puppy's way of playing. His story also gave me an alternate set of images about how I could react to the dogs' behavior. I could respond by playing with them. Having had only a limited exposure to dogs, I didn't know this before.

In ministry, God plays a significant part in supplying a supplicant with new images. God gives these through a variety of means: for instance, Scripture, discussion, the ministry of instruction, prophecy, a word of knowledge. Sometimes God gives these images directly to the supplicant, e.g. Larry "heard" God approve of him.

Often God gives images to the supplicant through the prayer team. In Larry's case, one team member received an image of God as Grandfather holding Larry as a child on his lap and rejoicing in him as only a grandparent can. She shared this image with Larry so that it became part of his changed perception of God as benevolent and of himself as a well-loved child of God.

When my father did a reconstruction of my experience, he used the phrase "pretend game" because I was too little to understand "imagine" or "visualize what happened." But into my imaginary replay of the original event, he introduced his own presence so that I would feel safe enough to try something new, even though it would be scary. In my imagination and with him present, he encouraged me to try out a new perception of these dogs' behavior. By pretending to play with one of them, I learned a new way of relating to dogs—with joy instead of terror. With my father's help, I began to "see" the dogs as playful rather than ferocious, and in my imagination I was able to pretend I was playing with one puppy, albeit timidly.

---

2. Chapter 6 of *Healing as a Parish Ministry* goes into greater detail about the importance of mental imagery and its use in prayer.

In ministry the team does something similar. Its physical presence to the supplicant while she is reliving a wounding experience gives her the support needed to relive the traumatic event. But the team does something that my father did not do. Into the mental replay of the traumatic event, the team introduces the presence of Jesus (or sometimes God as Parent). He is present to the supplicant as she relives the original trauma in a new way and with a different outcome. The presence of Jesus (or of God as Parent) does far more than make the supplicant feel safe, as my father's closeness did for me. Jesus' presence impacts us far more than any mere human presence can. Through Jesus, God's grace is brought into the reliving of the situation. Jesus indeed "rewrites the history of one's life," even though the *facts* of the original event remain the same. He "makes all things new." (TEV, Rev 21:5)

In the imaginative replay, Larry's father still made him wear a dunce cap at the dinner table, but the presence of Jesus changed the outcome and meaning of the original event. In the relived experience Jesus removed the dunce cap, consoled the humiliated Larry, and found a way to help him with his difficulty in school work. He helped Larry see that his father's cruelty came from his own emotional wounds. And just as the original experience of the event led Larry to feel—then act—dumb, the new experience conveyed through Christ's presence shaped Larry's future behavior. He no longer thought of himself as dumb and worthless. Instead, he recognized himself as a child of God, well loved and gifted by Him, approved by God. This is what Wise means by "reconstruction of the experience."

Emotional Healing is a Process

"Rewriting one's history" is a process that takes time. Usually many events and many people have contributed to a supplicant's wounded emotional life. To "rewrite" all of this history will take a number of sessions of bringing Christ's presence to bear on each important event and person.

Even when Jesus has dramatically healed a supplicant's wounded emotions, this healing needs to work itself into external behavior. After the pretend game, my father had me find the real dogs and play with them; then he got a dog for me. I started out in a mental process and ended up treasuring a pet dog. So too, in ministry, healing works from the inside out.

The phrase "healing an emotional wound" is deceptive because it makes healing sound too simple. With Larry, for example, years of ridicule had so damaged his self-image that it seriously affected his behavior. He thought of himself as incompetent and therefore behaved incompetently. After being healed of his image of himself as one who could not measure up, he had to learn how to behave as a well-loved child of God who had given him many talents. He needed time and help from others to make this behavioral change.

It takes time to break old patterns and to discover, and learn to use, these unrecognized talents. Therefore, most supplicants need long-term care when dealing with emotional wounds. The team may be the ones to help the person integrate her new self-image into her total way of life.

Frequently another need exists after an emotional wound has been healed. Emotional healing impacts supplicants' spiritual lives. They are freer than before to grow spiritually and may need help in doing so. Often they need guidance about their spiritual life, discipline, reading scripture, praying, carrying out their duties in life and relating to people in new ways.

Healing an emotional wound can have a dramatic effect on the life of a supplicant. Many experience it as a "new birth." Ministers are privileged to be present at such an event. They are witnessing a living-out of one of Christ's promises: "Look, I am making the whole of creation new." (NJB, Rev. 21:5a) In the face of such an event, ministers often recall the words of Yahweh to Moses at the burning bush: "Take off your sandals, for the place where you are standing is holy ground." (NJB, Ex 3:5)

A Note of Caution

Accounts of adults accusing others of sexually abusing them as children are becoming frequent and are sometimes highly publicized. Because healing ministers may encounter this issue in their ministry, I offer some cautions here.

Given the dual risks of lawsuits and of doing more harm than good in these matters, I believe that prayer teams should not attempt to minister emotional healing for sexual abuse unless they have had special, in-depth training for this problem.

Sometimes the supplicant is uncertain about an abusive event and wants the team to decide whether it really took place. I think the team should not attempt to do this. Even mental health professionals are not in agreement as to whether these memories are accurate accounts of actual events. If the team treats the event as being historically true when it isn't, they can seriously injure the accused. If they judge the event not to have happened when, in fact, it did, they can deprive the supplicant of the help he or she needs.

When a team tells someone they cannot meet a request, they must do so carefully so he or she will not feel rejected. I suggest that teams convey to their supplicant that they accept the seriousness of the issue, explain that this matter is beyond their expertise, then offer to refer the person to a competent, reliable person or specially trained prayer team.

For Further Reading

1. *Inner Healing*, by Michael Scanlan. Paulist Press, 1974.

2. *How to Pray for Inner Healing for Yourself and Others*, by Rita Bennett. Revel Co., 1984.

3. *Healing Life's Hurts: Healing Memories Through Five Stages of Forgiveness*, by Matthew and Dennis Linn. Paulist Press, 1978.

4. *Healing of Memories*, by Dennis and Matthew Linn. Paulist Press, 1974.

Summary—Chapter 8

A. Emotional healing through prayer ministry often takes place through a reconstruction of an experience, sometimes called "healing of memories" or "inner healing." The sequence is:

1. An experience that wounded someone in the past, especially in early childhood, affects his later behavior.

2. The event resides in the person's memory. Until it is healed, he is not free to respond as he would like and as he should. He is imprisoned by the earlier experience.

3. The wound is healed by bringing it into conscious memory and reliving it *in the light of Christ's healing presence.* When the original event is reconstructed, it is seen differently by the supplicant, has a different meaning for him and has a different outcome. This is the work of the Holy Spirit.

B. Healing emotional ills is a process

1. Many hurtful events, with many people involved, have contributed to a supplicant's wounded emotional life. Healing years of pain takes a number of sessions of bringing Christ's presence to bear on each important event and person.

2. Inner healing needs to work itself out into external behavior. It is a process that works from the inside out.

C. Emotional healing impacts a supplicant's spiritual life since he now is freer. To grow spiritually, he probably will need help, e.g. guidance about Scripture and prayer.

D. Caution: Prayer teams should not attempt to minister emotional healing for sexual abuse unless they have had special, in-depth training for this problem.

For Your Reflection—Chapter 8

1. Most of us have had unfortunate experiences, usually as children, that have damaged our perception of ourselves. Recall one such occasion in your life: create a mental "picture" of the event, then invite Jesus into that picture. Does he say something to you or to others? Does he do something? What deeper truth does he show you about this event that you find healing? ("You will know the truth, and the truth will set you free."—TEV, Jn 8:32) At the end of this reflection time, ask Jesus to lay his healing hands on you and bathe you in his love. What do you experience?

2. Ask yourself what emotion(s) you struggle with on an ongoing basis: resentment? fear? greed? In what way do these emotions block your relationship with God? How are they an obstacle to your becoming the person God wants you to be? Spend a few minutes in prayer, inviting the Holy Spirit to reveal to you what Jesus wants to do to remove these obstacles. Pay attention to your thoughts: What is God saying to you through them?

3. Sometimes we block the healing of our emotions by not believing that God wants to heal us of these wounds. Reflect on Psalm 34:18-20. How has God helped you, or someone you know, who is/has been "crushed in spirit"?

9

Healing Spiritual Wounds

❖   ❖   ❖   ❖   ❖

Sally was doubled over with emotional pain. She told me she
wished she'd never been born. She said she felt totally empty.
"My life has no meaning," she sobbed.

Sally, age 35, was married briefly in her twenties, and was
now divorced with no children. She had done graduate work at
an Ivy League University, but quit before she got her degree.
She grew up in a troubled home where her parents severely neglected her and her sister. Both parents had come from strict
religious families but had dropped all religious practices. Therefore, their children received no religious training. Sally's only
knowledge of religion came from two college courses: the com-
parative study of religions and the Bible as literature.

Recently Sally had expressed an interest in religion to an
acquaintance, who responded by taking her to a charismatic
prayer meeting. After the meeting, she went to the prayer ministry room and told a prayer team about how terribly empty she
felt. They prayed for healing of her childhood experience of pa-
rental neglect. She went back next week and told the team that
nothing had happened. They then told her they thought she
needed to "make a decision for Christ." The mere thought of
this frightened her. Sally fled in panic. Seeing her distress, her
friend suggested she ask me if I would talk to her.

Although Sally had a superior mind and many talents, when
she first visited me she was working in a restaurant as a dish
washer. In graduate school she had majored in ancient semitic
languages and for several years had worked as a research assistant

to a well-known scholar. She easily could have gotten work in this field, even without her degree. But she told me she no longer cared; she worked only to survive.

Sally's interest in religion came from a hope that it would fill the terrible emptiness she always felt and that it would take away her meaningless existence. But as we talked, I discovered that in Sally's mind, God was a dangerous person. She was so fearful of him that she couldn't pray or do religious things. The very thought of letting God have any control of her life terrified her. This explained why she had been so scared by the prayer team's attempt to get her to commit her life to Christ.

Sally's intelligence helped greatly in our work together. She was introspective and saw herself realistically. She recognized her intelligence and talents but said she couldn't believe she could do anything worthwhile. She drove herself to achieve goals but derived no enjoyment from her work. She said it seemed "worthless."

When we discussed her failed marriage she told me the central problem was love. "I can't experience love," she wept. "I feel unlovable. I can't love anyone. And sex scares me."

Further discussion surfaced other problems. Sally felt indifferent about her physical appearance, and failed to get medical attention when she needed it. She hoarded food and ate compulsively without enjoyment.

Although Sally had many emotional wounds that needed healing, I concluded that her primary wounds were spiritual. If my assessment was correct, emotional healing would not be effective until her spiritual wounds were healed. Sally's view of God as a terrifying person, her inability to experience love, her feelings of absolute emptiness and meaninglessness all pointed to spiritual woundedness.

I discussed my assessment with Sally and suggested that my ministry could focus on spiritual growth as well as healing of spiritual wounds. Sally liked this proposal, so we agreed to work together on her spirituality.

The Challenge of Spiritual Healing

Sally's experience with the prayer team illustrates the difficulty supplicants have in getting ministry for spiritual needs. On her second visit to the team, the ministers recognized her spiritual need, and made a clumsy attempt to meet it by asking her to "make a decision for Christ"—the very thing she was least able to do. The team's clumsiness is understandable. Until recently, the field of spirituality has been largely restricted to clergy. So the laity have lacked training in how to minister to spiritual needs. But this needs to change. Prayer teams must be trained to minister to spiritual wounds because *at the very least, a certain degree of spiritual woundedness is involved in every other kind of woundedness.*

But spiritual illness can be a hurt in its own right—a primary cause of woundedness. Severe forms, as in Sally's case, are often characterized by hopelessness, a lack of meaning to one's life, absolute emptiness and extreme loneliness. A spiritual wound may lie at the bottom of other hurts. Physical (as physicians are beginning to recognize), emotional and relational disturbances sometimes persist until a spiritual wound is healed.

In assessing a supplicant's needs, it is difficult to distinguish between emotional and spiritual hurts because both use the same channels—intellect, will and emotions—to express their symptoms. Nevertheless, the spiritual dimension differs from the emotional and deserves attention in its own right.

Healing prayer cannot meet every spiritual need of a supplicant. As with a person's physical life, there is a difference between growth, maintenance and healing in the spiritual life.

Growth

In the *physical order*, a child needs proper food and nurturing to become a fully adult human being. In the *spiritual order*, if a person is to become a mature Christian, he needs instruction about God, and a faith community that provides worship, ministry and conversion experiences.

Maintenance

In the *physical order*, once a person become a mature adult, she still needs a proper diet and exercise to maintain her healthy development. In the *spiritual order*, if a mature Christian wants to maintain her spiritual development, she must continue to be nourished by God's Word, by the Sacraments and by her faith community.

Healing

In the *physical order*, a broken bone needs to be set, placed in a cast and cared for in order to be healed. In the *spiritual order*, traumatic experiences and/or deprivations can so wound us that we cannot respond adequately to God's call to the fullness of life. Spiritual remedies are needed to heal spiritual wounds.

Christian Spirituality

> Everyone who does what is right has been begotten by God. See how much the Father has loved us! His love is so great that we are called God's children—and so in fact we are. (TEV, 1 Jn 3:1)

If we examine the above Scripture passage closely, it becomes clear that "spirituality" means more than doing holy things such as saying prayers and reading the Bible. John tells us that God has called us, through Christ, to become members of his family. Our part as adopted children is to respond to this call with the help of the Holy Spirit. We are to "do what is right." But to do that, we must "have the mind of Christ." (TEV, 1 Cor 2:16) The mind of Christ influences every thought, desire and action. From this comes our response. Every dimension of our being is involved!

In short, our spirituality is the totality of our life. *Every part of our life is part of our spirituality.* Spiritually, we can be more or less healthy. We are spiritually healthy when we are doing all we can, with God's grace, to respond to God's call. We are spiritually ill to the degree that our response to God's loving call is inadequate. Spiritual wounds (or hurts) are those things which prevent us from making an adequate response. This type of woundedness can be located in our mind when it does not conform with the mind of Christ, or in our will when our will does not conform with the will of the Father. Spiritual healing brings our mind into harmony with Christ's and our will into harmony with God's plan for us. Only then can we adequately respond to God's loving call to fullness of life.

Spiritual Ills Related to the Mind

There are a number of ways in which our minds can fail to conform with the mind of Christ. Four of these are lack of information, distorted information, worldly values and distorted self-image.

1. Lack of information

This is a common source of spiritual illness. Sally could not respond to God's call because, as a child, she had not been taught about God. She had never experienced God as a loving Parent.

Many of us suffer from this ill in a lesser way. I can have "head" knowledge about God and still lack "heart" knowledge. I can quote John 3:16, "God loved the world so much that he gave his only Son, so that everyone who believes in him may not die but have eternal life,"(TEV) but still find it difficult to believe that God loves *me*.

2. Distorted information

This is another common spiritual illness related to the mind. Sally thought of God as someone "out to get her." For her, God was a dangerous, terrifying person. Many of us suffer from a mild form of this kind of spiritual illness. For example, many Christians believe that God sends us sickness to test us or to chastise us.

3. Worldly values

Nearly everyone suffers from having adopted attitudes and values from the worldly culture we live in. For example, our culture teaches us to place so much of our security in money and possessions that it blocks us from trusting in God's care for us.

4. Distorted self-image

This is a nearly universal spiritual wound among those asking for healing prayer. Sally couldn't use her intelligence and other abilities because she thought she didn't amount to anything. She believed she couldn't do anything significant. A mental "tape" kept telling her, "You will never amount to anything; your parents were weird; you're weird; you can't do anything right."

Spiritual Ills Related to the Will

Our will can be hurt in such a way that we cannot make the kinds of choices that allow us to respond adequately to God's loving call. Two types of spiritual wounds of the will are compulsive behavior and an inability to love.

1. Compulsive behavior

Compulsive behavior troubles many supplicants. In spite of sincere and prolonged struggles, including the use of spiritual resources, many people are not free to make choices in the area of alcohol, drugs, sex, and food. Although not every wrong use in these areas is due to compulsion, many people are enslaved to addictions. Sally's use of food was compulsive.

2. Inability to love

The inability or unwillingness to love is a serious spiritual wound related to the will. Sally recognized this as the central problem in her failed marriage.

Sometimes the wound is a refusal to love. Closely associated with this is the inability or refusal to forgive. I recall a woman who professed to be a Christian but refused to see her daughter's children because the daughter married a man the woman disapproved of. When she came for ministry because of physical problems, this refusal to love turned out to be the root cause of her physical problems.

Resources for Spiritual Growth and Healing

Often a supplicant who needs spiritual healing also needs help with spiritual growth as well. This was true of Sally. I used a twofold plan for ministry with her: first, healing for her spiritual ills and, second, providing her with the means for spiritual growth.

Sally's ignorance of God and her distorted view of Him led me to decide that her greatest need was knowledge of God as a loving Parent who loved *her* personally. For this, I used the ministry of instruction. This was a teachable moment for Sally, so I arranged for her to meet weekly with Fr. Albert, a retired professor of theology, who was willing to instruct her in those truths of the faith that she needed at this moment of her life.

Sally's intelligence was an asset in her work with Fr. Albert. He enjoyed the challenge of a bright, eager student. She quickly learned a great deal of Christian theology.

But theoretical knowledge of God is never enough. I knew that Sally had to *experience* God as Loving Parent. Then she had to learn how to respond to this Loving Parent through prayer. To meet these needs, I taught Sally how to experience God through praying Scripture passages. In preparation for our weekly meetings, she read assigned passages from the Bible that portray God in a loving, nurturing way. One passage was Zeph. 3:16-17:

> Zion, have no fear, do not let your hands fall limp. Yahweh your God is in your midst, a victorious warrior. He will exult with joy over you, he will renew you by his love; he will dance with shouts of joy for you as on a day of festival. (JB)

At each meeting, Sally and I discussed her reaction to the passages or questions she had about their meaning. Then I read one of them to her, inserting her name in place of Zion, or Daughter, to make it more personal. We spent some time in silence before I would ask her what she was experiencing. Then we discussed that. Gradually she came to experience God as a loving and caring parent who loved her personally. After I had taught Sally this method of praying Scripture, she continued it on her own and often commented on the power of Scripture to transform her life.

As she progressed in the spiritual life, I taught Sally to meditate on the life of Jesus and to use the prayer of praise—especially during times of discouragement and difficulty.

After Sally felt more comfortable with God, I arranged for her to have weekly sessions with a prayer team. They prayed for healing of her wounded emotional life stemming from her early childhood experiences. They also prayed for healing of her terror of God, and for ridding her of her mental "tapes" that said she couldn't do anything worthwhile. Sally reported that the team's ministry was effective. She especially valued their use of blessed oil and laying on of hands. But best of all, the team made generous use of the prayer of affirmation. As a result of their ministry, she resumed her graduate studies and eventually became a recognized scholar in the area of biblical languages.

About six months after beginning prayer ministry, Sally decided to become a Christian. In preparation for this, the prayer team helped her forgive her parents for their lack of care for her. This was quite hard for her to do. The team encouraged her to make daily use of the aspiration "Lord Jesus, I place my parents in the cathedral of your heart." While praying this way, Sally, in her imagination, saw her parents being received by Jesus, embracing them and loving them. Then Jesus called her into the scene and told her that she had failed in love, too, since she was harboring bitterness toward them for their failures. He then asked her to forgive them and to repent of her bitterness and lack of love, and to ask their forgiveness. In the mental scene, she did so and they embraced. In real life, she reestablished a relationship with her parents, from whom she had been estranged. This helped heal her of her inability to love others.

At Easter, Sally was baptized, confirmed and received Holy Communion. This was a major turning point in her life. The ceremony of Baptism gave her a sense of a new beginning and of belonging to a community of people. Several years later she told me she still had a lot of emotional pain, but since being baptized she had never felt that utter emptiness and meaninglessness of her life. "I now know that I have a destiny," she said. She received Holy Communion often and found it to be a healing sacrament. When receiving Communion she would ask Jesus to heal some part of her that still seemed wounded, and she experienced Jesus touching and healing her inner being.

Follow-Up Ministry

Several weeks after her baptism, Sally said she felt well enough to discontinue weekly ministry. I agreed with her, but told her that I thought she needed to maintain her healing and to grow in her spiritual life. The healing that had taken place in Sally's inner being now needed to percolate out into her external way of life. This would take time, plus the help of others.

Because I was about to move to a new assignment, I could not do follow-up ministry. However, Fr. Albert was delighted to offer this ministry to Sally. He agreed to see her once a month and be available if she was having a difficult time. Sally kept in touch with me through an occasional letter and mutual friends and told me that Fr. Albert had helped her become active in the parish in which she had been baptized.

A key element of follow-up ministry is belonging to a stable faith community that possesses the resources needed for both maintenance and growth. This usually means being a member of a parish or congregation. The healed supplicant needs to live in a context of faith, hope and love. She needs the inspiration provided by fellow Christians attempting to be faithful followers of Christ.

In addition to her parish faith community, Fr. Albert encouraged Sally to make a Cursillo and to become active in that movement. This gave her a smaller and more intimate group with which to share her life. It also met another need: that of regular accountability. Being accountable to another or to a group is a powerful way to help inner healing percolate out into one's every day behavior.

Sometimes follow-up takes the form of an opportunity for offering meaningful Christian service. After a year of follow-up ministry, Fr. Albert raised this issue with Sally. She decided to do volunteer work with severely developmentally disabled children.

Fr. Albert kept in touch with Sally about her prayer life and taught her new ways of praying at the proper time so that she would continue to progress in her ability to pray. After about a year with Fr. Albert, Sally had to move to a new location and felt that she was able to continue to live her spiritual life without any special help. She continues to be serious about her spiritual journey and is living a happy and productive Christian life.

Conclusion

Paul said God "gave us the task of making others his friends. . . ." (TEV, 2 Cor 5:18b) Faced with exercising the ministry of spiritual healing, we may be held back by a reluctance to tread on someone's spiritual turf. But *each* of us has been called to this ministry to some degree. We need to discern to what degree we are called and for whom.

Spiritual healing is a demanding ministry because, to do it well, we must be well-educated in spiritual matters. Also, we need to have a deep, mature personal relationship with God. On the plus side, it is in the ministry of spiritual healing that I experience God more powerfully than in any other area of my life. More than anything else I do, this ministry reveals to me the transforming power of God's love.

For Further Reading

1. *Behold Your God,* by Agnes Sanford. MacAlester Park Publishing Co., 1958.

2. *On the Road to Spiritual Wholeness: Life Signs and Danger Signals,* by Flora Slosson Wuellner. Abingdon, 1978.

Summary—Chapter 9

A. A certain degree of spiritual woundedness is involved in every other kind of woundedness, but spiritual illness can also be a primary wound. Both emotional and spiritual wounds use the intellect, will and emotions to express themselves.

B. In the spiritual life, there is a difference between *growth, maintenance* and *healing:*

   1. *Growth:* To become a mature Christian, a person needs instruction about God, plus a faith community.

   2. *Maintenance:* A mature Christian must continue to be nourished by God's word, the sacraments and the faith community.

   3. *Healing:* Traumatic experiences and/or deprivation can leave us unable to respond to God's call to the fullness of life.

C. Spiritual ills related to the *mind* include:

   1. *Lack of information*

   2. *Distorted information*

   3. *Worldly values*

   4. *Distorted self-image*

D. Spiritual ills related to the *will* include:

   1. *Compulsive behavior*

   2. *Inability to love*

E. Follow-up ministry is a vital part of spiritual healing. It should include belonging to a stable faith community that possesses the resources needed for maintenance and growth.

   1. Accountability to the community is one way for healing to enter into a supplicant's everyday life.

   2. Christian service can be a form of follow-up ministry.

For Your Reflection—Chapter 9

1. Every person has some image of what and who God is. In this chapter, Sally thought of God as a dangerous person. Some people use words like "distant and impersonal" or "warm and caring" when asked to describe God. Make a list of words that express *your* ideas and feelings about God. How many of these words fit with the type of person you would feel safe with? How many of them hinder your relationship with God?

2. Think of an occasion when you became spiritually wounded. For instance, when you were a child someone may have given you wrong information about God. Review the summary for this chapter, then reflect on whether your wound seems to have arisen primarily from the mind (e.g., an emphasis on worldly values, distorted self-image) or the will (e.g., compulsive behavior). Ask Jesus to come and make his love for you more real. What do you experience?

3. Read Zephaniah 3:16-17 several times, each time inserting your name in place of "Zion." Scripture has many places where God calls the People of Israel by name (e.g., Zion, Jerusalem, Israel, Jacob). Each time you run across one of these names while reading the Bible, substitute your own name. Listen to God calling *you* by name! "See, upon the palms of my hands I have written your name." (NAB, Is 49:16)

10

Healing Wounded Relationships

❖ ❖ ❖ ❖ ❖

I had known Ida a long time. She and her life-long friend, Vivian, were both widows in their 60's who now shared a house together. After they had been living together several months, Ida came to me in tears, saying "I've never been so hurt in my entire life."

The day before, Vivian had exploded in anger as Ida sat reading while Vivian vacuumed. Out of the blue, Vivian had shouted, "You lazy slob! I wished to hell I'd never met you!" Then she accused Ida of just sitting around the house expecting her to clean up after her. Shocked, Ida had started to cry. Then she got mad and told Vivian she was sick and tired of her always "fussing around," moving her things and sticking them in drawers so she couldn't find them. Ida called Vivian an "old mother hen."

Ida came to me saying she was furious with Vivian but didn't want to keep on hating her the way she did right then. "We've been good friends since we were kids," she said, "and I don't want to lose this friendship." Ida asked me to help her set things right between her and Vivian.

Relationships are not optional for human beings. From birth to death, we depend upon others for our very existence. Without satisfying, nurturing relationships we can become sick and may even die. A surviving spouse sometimes loses the will to live and dies soon after the death of a marriage partner. Important relationships are vital to our well-being.

But, like Ida, we sometimes badly manage our important relationships, such as those with our parents, children, spouses, friends, working partners. Then these relationships become a destructive force in our lives, causing us hurts that need healing.

Sometimes a person with wounded relationships seeks help from a prayer team as Ida did. A knowledge of the many sources of hurt in a relationship will aid the team in devising a plan of action to bring healing to the relationship. Here are six common sources of hurt.

Sources of Hurt in Relationships

1. Violation of Explicit Agreements

Sometimes people make explicit agreements with others, then violate those agreements. Even if an agreement is broken because of changing circumstances, it can cause much hurt. For instance, during their engagement a couple decided they'd have children soon after marriage, and the wife would quit working. However, after the birth of the first child, the husband decided to return to college. This meant his wife had to go back to work and place the child in day care. The woman was not in agreement with this plan and felt her husband had gone back on his agreement. Their relationship rapidly deteriorated.

2. Violation of Unexpressed Expectations

Our expectations of another are frequently unexpressed. Sometimes we ourselves are unaware of them. We form these expectations early in life by adopting the attitudes of people important to us, especially our parents. Unthinkingly, we come to believe that their way of relating to others is the only "right" way. Unconscious expectations wield great power over our behavior. They have the quality of "You *must* meet my expectation."

For example, a recently married woman came for ministry because she was upset with her husband. She said that although her husband was very loving, generally thoughtful, and helpful in many ways, he absolutely refused to do any work in the kitchen. He would not even fix a snack or make coffee for himself but expected her to do it for him. She resented this behavior, saying he expected her to be his slave. He, on the other hand, insisted that this was "woman's work."

In looking at their early family experiences, it turned out the husband came from a rural family that sharply divided the roles of men and women. His father, mother and both sets of grandparents believed that preparing food was women's work. The husband could not even conceive of any other arrangement. The wife, on the other hand, had come from an urban family in which both parents shared equally in all the home tasks, including food preparation. She, too, could not conceive of any other arrangement. Both believed that the other had violated an agreement, when in fact it was only an unexpressed expectation that each had of the other. They had not discussed their expectations before marriage.

3. Conflicts and Quarrels

People in relationships have different needs and desires. Sometimes these clash. Conflict in itself is not hurtful. It can lead to maturity and growth in a relationship. But sometimes the parties cannot find a constructive way to resolve a conflict. They end up quarreling and blaming the other as Vivian and Ida did (at the beginning of this chapter).

When Ida could discuss the quarrel more calmly, it became apparent that literature and needlework were important to her and that she spent a great deal of time with both. The appearance of the house was not very important to her, and never had been even in her former home.

On the other hand, Vivian loved a beautiful home and cheerfully spent a lot of time cleaning and decorating. But she resented Ida's lack of cooperation in housekeeping. Only dimly aware of these different desires, they had not attempted to reach a mutually agreeable resolution to this conflict of interests and had ended up calling each other names.

4. Immature Relationships

Immaturity or inner woundedness can cause us to act destructively in important relationships, such as husband-wife, parent-child, friendships, and in relationships with institutions such as the church. The destructiveness takes many forms, e.g. excessive dependency upon the other, dominating the other, physical and sexual abuse, jealousy, and possessiveness.

For instance, a husband seeks ministry because his wife's jealous behavior baffles him. He reports a typical incident where he and his wife were dining with another couple in a restaurant. While taking their order, the waitress—previously unknown to any of them—called him "my dear." His wife stood up and shouted at the waitress "He is not '*your* dear;' he's '*my* dear' and don't you forget it!" He and the other couple were mortified at this outburst.

5. Intentional hurts

Intentional cruelty can cause the most painful wounds, and may be the most difficult to heal. When I was chaplain in a hospital, I visited an elderly woman who had been badly beaten by a young man who had broken into her apartment to rob her. She was physically incapable of preventing the robbery. The intruder had beaten her for no reason except sadistic pleasure. She told me she could forgive the man for robbing her because she knew what it was to need money. But she found it hard to forgive his deliberate cruelty. This example of intentional cruelty is extreme, but the deliberate use of cruel remarks, racial slurs, and put-downs are common, even among family and friends.

6. Unintentional Hurts

Even unintentional events can seriously wound relationships. I remember an accident in my childhood that shattered our neighborhood. During a game of "cops and robbers," John, age ten, was shot and killed by a playmate, Harold, who thought the gun he was playing with was empty. Everyone knew it was unintentional, but John's parents blamed Harold's parents and refused to forgive either Harold or his parents. We kids felt torn. Not knowing how to relate to Harold, we mostly avoided him. Out of hurt, Harold's family eventually moved away from the neighborhood.

The Challenge of Healing Wounded Relationships

Occasionally both parties to a wounded relationship - husband and wife, parents and child, friend and friend, even entire families—seek ministry from a prayer team. Teams can minister to them as a unit, but the more common arrangement is to minister to each person individually. Most often, however, only one of the parties asks for help. The rest of this chapter focuses on ministering to an individual in need of relational healing.

Healing a wounded relationship almost always involves emotional and spiritual healing. (See Chapters 8 and 9) But special considerations exist in relational healing. For example, ministry may reveal a supplicant's need to change his expectations of another, to give up his own viewpoint as the only way to look at things and accept the other's as equally valid. Or a supplicant may need to look honestly at his own immaturity and do some growing up. This might mean making use of a psychological or spiritual counselor.

The team should keep two elements in mind as they minister relational healing.

- This ministry provides the supplicant with a unique opportunity to discover, and repent of, personal sin in his way of relating to others.
- It exposes the supplicant's need to forgive others or to seek their forgiveness.

Steps in Healing a Wounded Relationship

As with other types of healing, relational healing usually occurs in steps, not in one, big leap. Common steps in healing a wounded relationship are:

1. The team helps the supplicant affirm (or reaffirm) that Jesus is Lord of her life. This is best done in the form of a prayer in which the supplicant invites Jesus to be Lord of her life here and now.

Such a declaration may not come easily. In the face of a difficult situation, to reaffirm an earlier decision that Jesus' way of love is to be her rule of life may test the supplicant's sincerity and precipitate some soul-searching. She may need the team's help to meet this challenge for growth in her spiritual life.

Some supplicants have never deliberately, consciously invited Jesus to be Lord of their life. These people may need considerable help from the team. They may need some explanation of what making Jesus Lord will mean in their daily life. The team might recommend a book and then discuss it with them. The team might recommend that a supplicant attend a Life in the Spirit seminar, make a Cursillo or a retreat. This first step needs to be taken, even if it means deferring prayer for healing the relationship for some time.

To ask someone to make Jesus Lord of her life when she has never considered this before, is to ask her to make a radical change in her life. It may expose much else that needs to be done before the wounded relationship can be healed. If the team thinks of its ministry solely as praying rather than of caring for the total person, it likely will skip over this first step and start immediately to pray for healing.

A team inexperienced in pastoral care may find it difficult to talk to the supplicant about such intimate spiritual matters. To them, it may feel like an invasion of the person's privacy, so they skip over this first step. This delicate pastoral task must be handled sensitively, but it is the foundation of all else that happens in this ministry and must *not* be passed over! To neglect it may render any other prayer ministry useless.

2. The team helps the supplicant explicitly invite Jesus to be Lord of **this** *relationship that is wounded.* This is best done in the form of a prayer. This may be the first time the supplicant has thought about Jesus being Lord of a *relationship*; she may need help to think through what this will mean. But even if she is reaffirming an earlier decision, as in a marriage, there will be something new

about it this time, e.g. some new growth, or a giving over of some
new thing to Jesus as Lord of this relationship in *this* situation.

To help a supplicant release her hurt feelings about the
other person in the wounded relationship, I sometimes suggest
to the supplicant the following method of prayer:

- Ask the supplicant to bring to mind some image of the
  Heart of Jesus—perhaps a spacious and beautiful cathedral
  filled with love.
- Then, ask the supplicant to start using the aspiration "Jesus!
  I place (name) in the cathedral of your heart." She should
  do this for several minutes in a relaxed way, in rhythm with
  her breathing.
- Ask the supplicant to attempt to bring the other person into
  the imagined scene and perhaps even see or hear or feel
  what Jesus is doing in regard to the other person. After
  praying this way for a few minutes, she may sense Jesus addressing her (the supplicant), saying something like "Be
  compassionate as I am compassionate" or "I have given my
  life that (name) may have life."

*3. The team leads the supplicant into repenting of his own part in the
wounding of the relationship.* The supplicant may need to give up
his unrealistic and demanding expectations of the other person.
Perhaps, upon reflection, he can see his immaturity expressed in
possessiveness, overdependence, or jealousy. Or perhaps, he has
taken the other for granted and not valued him or her as a gift
from God. Each of these insights are invitations from the Lord
to spiritual growth, i.e. repentance. A supplicant often starts out
seeking how he can forgive the other in this wounded relationship, and find that he needs to ask the other for forgiveness.

In asking someone for forgiveness, it is best for the supplicant to say explicitly, "Will you forgive me for (name the of-
fense)?" The clarity of the question lets the other person know
that he wants to heal the relationship. It identifies for him what
the supplicant thinks has wounded their bond. It is also important for the one being asked for forgiveness to make a clear response, such as, "Yes I do forgive you," or "I need to talk this
over with you first," or "I need some time to handle this, but I'll

get back to you." When someone is asked for forgiveness, it is unhelpful to brush it off by saying something like "It wasn't anything" or "It didn't matter."

There are exceptions to this direct approach. Some people cannot handle emotionally charged situations. Talking about forgiveness embarrasses them and is counterproductive. In these cases, it is better to use some symbolic action to indicate the wish to make amends, such as a gift or card. Putting a person in a situation they cannot handle is an unloving thing to do.

During ministry a supplicant may discover she needs to forgive someone—even without being asked—for hurts that person has inflicted. Forgiving another is a two-step process: making a decision to forgive, and letting go of the emotions of anger and hurt. The steps already mentioned in making Jesus Lord of the relationship usually enable the supplicant to forgive the other person.

The Challenge of Forgiveness

Sometimes a supplicant finds it seemingly impossible to forgive. This difficulty may indicate the need for healing of memories. The inner wounds may be so raw that they block forgiveness. Once the memories are healed, forgiveness can take place.

But difficulty in forgiving may also indicate the need to give up unrealistic expectations of the other person. The supplicant usually is unconscious of holding onto these unrealistic expectations and will need help to become aware of them—perhaps with the help of a psychological counselor.

I remember a woman named Ursula who came to our prayer team seeking inner healing. She was a deeply spiritual woman, devoted to helping crippled children. She told us she was emotionally scarred from being raised in a physically violent and chaotic family. She said she wanted help in getting over the anger she felt towards her mother. They quarreled whenever they talked. In spite of repeated efforts, she felt unable to forgive her mother for having been such an uncaring mother.

Discussion made it clear that the mother had been mentally ill during Ursula's childhood, and in fact still was ill. Further discussion made it clear Ursula could not forgive her mother because she held on to the expectation that her mother *should* have loved her then and *should* love her even now. This expectation had the quality of a demand. Given the mother's mental illness, this was totally unrealistic. Unconsciously, Ursula was withholding her forgiveness in an attempt to force her mother to love her. With the prayer team's help, Ursula admitted that her mother was incapable of loving others. She then was able to release her unrealizable expectation and to forgive her mother for the wounds caused by being deprived of maternal love.

When a supplicant is having difficulty forgiving another, a team may need to instruct him in methods of prayer that facilitate forgiveness. (Three books I recommend are listed at the end of this chapter.)

I personally use the prayer of praise when I find it difficult to forgive someone. I praise God for this person, or this situation, and even for the hurt of this relationship. I can do this with sincerity because of my conviction that God will bring good out of even sinful situations.

I also use the prayer of thanksgiving. I thank God for the gift this person is to others or has been to me. I thank God for all the gifts He has given to this person. When I am having great difficulty in forgiving, I ask God to bless this person's ministry twice as much as He blesses mine. I usually find all of this hard to do in the beginning, but if I force myself to say the words, I soon find that I can say them with some degree of sincerity. What begins as a clenched-jaw act of will ends in a real change of heart. Over time I have observed that God does answer this prayer and has blessed the ministry of the other more than mine. I find it amazing that through a struggle to gain a forgiving heart, God is glorified and the Body of Christ is built up!

Pastoral Cautions

We live in an age of pop psychology that believes that conflicts are best settled by talking about how we feel about things. Sometimes this is true, but not always. Sometimes it just muddles things even more. This is especially true when neither party is healed sufficiently to forgive the other. Also, as mentioned earlier, some people are not skilled or comfortable in talking about feelings. They prefer to heal a relationship by indirect means or by a symbolic action, such a giving a gift. Their intention behind this style of seeking reconciliation should be respected as genuinely loving.

The greatest potential danger in the area of forgiveness is to equate *forgiveness* with *restoration of the relationship*. They are *not* the same! To forgive is to once again direct our love toward a person from whom we have withdrawn it. Ideally this should lead to reestablishing the relationship to its former status. But it is not always possible or even a loving thing to do. We must always forgive, but not always restore the relationship. Much harm is done when these two things are confused.

For instance, Emma sought help from a prayer team when she discovered that her husband was sexually abusing their eldest daughter. On the advice of a social worker, Emma and the children were living apart from the father. Through the team's ministry, Emma experienced considerable healing of the hurt. After much internal struggle, she finally let go of the bitterness she felt towards her husband and forgave him. However, the team mistakenly told her that forgiveness must include restoration of the relationship. Even though the social worker told her not to allow the husband alone with the daughter, Emma followed the team's instruction and returned with the children to live with her husband. Tragically the sexual abuse of the daughter resumed. Restoring the relationship was not a loving act for the husband, the daughter, or Emma.

Conclusion

A wounded relationship can impact every other aspect of a supplicant's life because, by nature, people are relational beings. The need for relational healing often is interwoven with the need for emotional and spiritual healing. A team that encounters all these needs within one supplicant may feel as though they're trying to unsnarl a delicate gold chain that's gotten tangled up over a period of time. Teams that feel overwhelmed need to remember the cycle of ministry (Chapter 3) and the eight ingredients in prayer ministry (Chapter 2). Within these structures, teams will find that prayer, patience, love and discernment can help free people from the bondage of wounded relationships.

For Further Reading

1. *Learning to Forgive,* by Doris Donnelly. Abingdon Press, 1979.
2. *Forgive and Forget: Healing the Hurts We Don't Deserve,* by Lewis B. Smedes. Harper and Row, 1984.

Summary—Chapter 10

A. Important relationships can become a destructive force in our lives. Common sources of hurt are: Violation of explicit agreements, violation of unexpressed expectations, conflicts and quarrels, immature relationships, intentional hurts, and unintentional hurts.

B. Special challenges exist in relational healing, including:

1. Supplicants often need to discover, and repent of, personal sin as regards their way of relating to others.

2. Relational healing exposes the supplicant's need to forgive others or to seek their forgiveness.

C. Common steps in ministering to relational wounds are:

1. The team helps the supplicant affirm (or reaffirm) that Jesus is Lord of his life.

2. The team helps the supplicant explicitly invite Jesus to be Lord of *this* relationship that is wounded.

3. The team leads the supplicant into repenting of his own part in the wounding of the relationship.

D. Forgiveness is a special challenge in relational healing.

1. Blocks to forgiveness can include a need for healing of memories or a need to give up unrealistic expectations.

2. Teams can instruct a supplicant in methods of prayer that facilitate forgiveness, including prayer of praise and prayer of thanksgiving.

3. Forgiveness is *not* the same as restoration of a relationship! The former should always be a goal of ministry, but the latter may not be possible or may not be advisable.

For Your Reflection—Chapter 10

1. Think of someone with whom you have a wounded relationship, then look at the first part of the chapter summary. What seems to have been the main source of hurt in that relationship? (e.g. violation of explicit agreements such as wedding promises? unintentional hurts such as accidental injury?) Visualize Jesus coming into a painful moment in this relationship and hear/see what he has to say to *each* of you. Where does the other person need to grow? Where do you need to grow?

2. To continue with the same individual in Question #1: If you feel ready to do so, ask Jesus to come to you with a gift—the gift of forgiveness of that person. If you do not feel ready for this step, ask Jesus to give you the *desire* to forgive him/her.

3. Giving up a hurt can be even more painful than forgiving someone. Read Lk 22:54-62. Put yourself in Jesus' place and imagine the hurt he felt as one of his closest friends denied even knowing him. Then read Jn 21:15-19. Jesus says, "Peter, do you love me?" then entrusts to him the sacred task of continuing the mission that he (Jesus) has begun. Could Jesus have done this if he had clung to the hurt of Peter's denial? If you think you are in some way still holding onto the hurt inflicted on you by the person in Questions #1 and 2, ask Jesus for the grace to give up that hurt. Ask him for the gift of freedom.

11

Healing a Wounded Relationship With God

❖   ❖   ❖   ❖   ❖

This was Susan's first meeting with the parish prayer team. When the team leader asked her what she was seeking ministry for, she blurted out, "I am so angry with God that I would spit in his face if I could see him!" The prayer team sat in silence, stunned at the vehemence of her outburst. Susan began crying in embarrassment, saying, "I shouldn't have said that."

Supplicants frequently harbor negative feelings towards God. They may be angry with God, feeling He has treated them unfairly; or they may be disappointed, feeling God has let them down when they needed him most. Supplicants may resist expressing anger towards God because, like Susan, they know they "shouldn't feel this way." They also may fear what the team will think of them for having such feelings. So teams need to routinely explore whether or not a supplicant has these feelings and then help her express them.

Team members reverence God and therefore may have difficulty allowing a supplicant to speak of God in negative ways. As with Susan's team, they may be shocked; or they may rush to God's defense and rebuke the supplicant. A few misguided Christians react in horror, believing the supplicant has committed an "unforgivable" sin of "blaspheming the Holy Spirit" (Mt 12:32).[1]   But if a wounded relationship between a supplicant and

---

1.   In Mt 12:22, the Pharisees saw Jesus cure "a blind and dumb demoniac" and

God is to be healed, the voicing of negative feelings must be accepted by the supplicant and the team. Only then can the root problem behind the feelings be located and healed.

The techniques for ministering to a wounded relationship apply to healing a wounded relationship with God. But eventually the hurt also will have to be dealt with as a spiritual wound. Usually the immediate cause is a tragedy, such as the death of a loved one, a serious illness, or a financial hardship. Almost always, however, the root cause is a combination of an immature relationship with God, plus unrealistic expectations of him.

Immature Understanding of God

We have been taught that God is all-knowing and all-powerful. But we may not have been taught that God chose to heal and bless us through accepting the limitation of His becoming human. This is the meaning of the Incarnation. This is the mystery of the Cross. People who have not been taught this understanding of God's way of acting in the world often see Him as a giant puppeteer, where every creature in the world is connected to God by a string; God manipulates each creature to bring about every event. This view of God and the universe leads people to say, "God has taken my loved one away from me." Or, "God has sent this painful illness upon me."[2] They feel God is unloving, and respond with hurt feelings towards Him.

---

declared the work evil. It was their persistent refusal to respond to God—the closing of their hearts—that Jesus called blasphemy against the Holy Spirit. Anger with God is not a turning away from Him. It's a form of going *towards* Him with feelings of pain and distress.

2. Church authorities, leaders and/or teachers sometimes fuel this misunderstanding of God's way of acting in the world. For instance, in an article in *America*, William O'Malley asserts that the sacrament of healing is not meant for healing; rather it is a grace that empowers us to do what Jesus did—"die and survive": "One of the holiest men I've met, a merchant seaman dying alone of cancer and tuberculosis, said it most eloquently: 'Yes, it is very difficult. But isn't it wonderful God trusts me enough to give it to me?'" (O'Malley, William J. "Understanding the Sacraments." *America*: Vol. 166, No. 8 (March 7, 1992), p. 188.)

This immature understanding of God—which actually is a spiritual wound—is the root cause of wounded relationships with God. It has to be corrected before the relationship can be healed. All the resources discussed in the chapter on healing spiritual wounds should be used.

A wounded relationship with God also contains elements of emotional woundedness. A supplicant's relationship with God may have been wounded by some traumatic event. For instance, Susan's anger at God arose when her husband and infant son died in a house fire. Teams should treat this type of trauma as an emotional wound and use all the resources available for emotional healing. It can be very healing to reconstruct the experience by use of the imagination and let God speak through the ministry of the team.

In Susan's case, the team gently led her back, in memory, to the fire that killed her husband and child. In prayer they brought Jesus' presence into that scene; Jesus held Susan and wept with her at the tragedy of her husband and child being killed in the fire. After several sessions like this, she was able to release her bitterness toward God and forgive him and ask for his forgiveness for thinking so badly of him. Also, through instruction by the team Susan came to a more mature understanding of the nature of God and his relationship to his creatures.

Wounded Relationships with the Church

One day while I was at a dry cleaners in my black suit and roman collar, a woman named Ruby asked me if I was a Lutheran minister. I responded that I was a Roman Catholic priest and asked if she was Lutheran. She said, "No, I was a Catholic once. But a priest treated us so badly when Grandmother died that I said 'to hell with the Church.' I'm nothing now." I told her I was sorry to hear she had been treated so badly and asked if I could be of help in resolving things. She said, "Maybe," so I gave her my card. When Ruby phoned later, I arranged for her to meet with a prayer team for ministry.

Ruby's story is a common one. Many supplicants have a wounded relationship with the Church. Often someone who represents the Church has done something—or failed to do something—that has caused them hurt. As they perceive it, it is not just a *person* who has hurt them, it is the *Church*. Because the Church is an institution whose structures are sometimes impersonal, they don't know how to heal and restore the wounded relationship. A prayer team representing the church can act in the name of the church and bring about healing and reconciliation.

Ruby's team used the standard methods of praying for healing of emotional wounds. They had Ruby return to the painful memory of the priest being unhelpful at the time of her grandmother's death and then invoked the presence of Jesus. At one crucial point in the process of reconciliation between Ruby's family and the priest, the team leader stood in proxy for the priest and asked Ruby's forgiveness. The action enabled Ruby to forgive the Church by forgiving the team leader. Ruby's former relationship with the Church was restored.

Conclusion

For us to be instruments of healing a wounded relationship with God, we ourselves must have a realistic, mature relationship with Him. We must be able to acknowledge the reality of *all* emotional responses towards God, including feelings of anger. Teams that reject such feelings—their own or a supplicant's—will block healing. Teams that allow the expression of all feelings will enable their supplicants to move into a deeper relationship with God, one that includes the full range of their emotions.

For Further Reading

1. *May I Hate God?*, by Pierre Wolff. Paulist Press, 1979.

Summary—Chapter 11

A. Supplicants frequently harbor negative feelings towards God. These usually arise from a combination of:

1. A non-incarnational view of God that sees him as a Divine Puppeteer, i.e., the manipulator of all that is good *and* bad. This is a spiritual wound and eventually needs to be treated as such.

2. A response to some traumatic event. This is an emotional wound and should be dealt with accordingly.

B. Many supplicants have a wounded relationship with the Church, arising from the actions, or inactions, of someone who represents the Church. A prayer team representing the Church can act in the name of the Church to bring about healing and reconciliation. Often this will include speaking on behalf of the Church to ask the supplicant's forgiveness.

C. Prayer ministers need to have their own mature relationship with God in order to be able to accept the whole spectrum of a supplicant's emotional feelings about God.

For Your Reflection—Chapter 11

1. Do you sometimes see God as a Divine Puppeteer, pulling the strings of your life to cause both positive *and* negative things to happen to you and your loved ones? For a different view of God, read Lk 2:1-7. Imagine Jesus' vulnerability in this scene in Bethlehem, his dependency on people for survival. Then read Lk 23:33-46, where Jesus' vulnerability is mocked, scorned and abused. Pray for the gift of being able to bow to the mystery that God is both vulnerable *and* all-powerful.

2. Recall an occasion where some representative of the Church wounded you by his/her action or inaction (pastor? nun? minister? Sunday school teacher?). Ask Jesus to come into that memory. What do you sense him saying to the person

who hurt you? What do you sense him saying to you? If you are willing to do so, ask Jesus to bless and heal the one who hurt you. Then ask him to bless and heal this particular wound of yours.

3. Holy people in Scripture sometimes expressed anger towards God. Jeremiah had two crises of faith where he raged at God: "Truly, for me you are a deceptive stream with uncertain waters!" (JB, Jer 15:18b), and "You duped me, O Lord, and I let myself be duped" (NAB, Jer 20:7a). Think of a time when you experienced a crisis in your relationship with God. Were you able to express negative feelings to Him? If you were unable to do so then, go back in your memory to that time and feel God's unconditional acceptance of you, including *all* your feelings about Him.

12

Unrecognized Ministries

❖   ❖   ❖   ❖   ❖

Ministers of religious healing often forget that God has given us many ways to minister to human hurts. If we restrict our pastoral care solely to prayer, we miss other ways of bringing God's healing touch to hurting people.

This chapter describes four traditional Christian ministries that can be powerful means of healing. They are: extending hospitality, comforting, accepting self-disclosure, and giving instruction. Many ministers have helped others in these ways but perhaps have never thought of them as forms of ministry. Recognizing these and consciously making them a part of ministry expands the ways in which we can help others.

Extending Hospitality

One day when my lifelong friend, Bill, and I were talking on the phone, he told me I sounded depressed and unhappy. I admitted he was right. I said I was feeling lonely, and my career seemed to be at a standstill. I felt I needed to change directions, but I didn't know where to go or what I'd do next. Plus, I said, "I'm physically worn out and feeling overwhelmed."

Bill responded by saying it sounded like I could use a change of scene to sort things out. He invited me to come visit him and his family in another city, saying that his wife, Mary, and his children would be glad to see me, and so would he.

I accepted Bill's invitation and stayed with him several weeks. While there, I played with his children, worked in the garden, got extra rest and usually took a long walk each day. I found a counselor who helped me sort out important issues and pinpoint the decisions I needed to make. I found a spiritual director who helped me hear the Lord's call.

I did not use my friend for any of this, and when we were together, I seldom even talked about it with him. We talked about old friends, watched TV together, and mostly just enjoyed each others' company. The counselor and spiritual director helped me make the decisions needed to put my life in order, but the hospitality of Bill and his family made this possible.

I'm sure the idea of ministry never crossed Bill's mind. He did not lay hands on me or pray over me, but he gave me precisely what I needed and could not get anywhere else. He ministered hospitality to me. He made space for me in his home, family and heart. Through Bill and his family, I received the peace of Christ that carried me forward in my spiritual journey. At that time, no one else could have done that for me. The ministry flowed out of a unique relationship between Bill and me.

All Christian ministry must flow out of a relationship. Jesus is the mediator between God and us. He is our point of contact with God. Now that he has ascended into heaven, Jesus continues to be our mediator, but he acts *through* us, his Body. We make up the Body of Christ. He is the head, we the members. We are the mouth of Christ and the hands of Christ. When we, in Christ's name, lay hands upon a woman, Christ touches her through us. When we, in Christ's name, speak words of comfort to a man, Christ comforts him through us. When Bill gave me the space in which to catch my breath, Christ showed me hospitality.

The biblical notion of hospitality as a sacred duty was based on the Israelites' nomadic life. Deserts teem with hazards, and the desert traveler cannot survive unless those he meets will offer him food, water and rest in a place of safety. Genesis 18 describes Abraham as the biblical model of a host. Sitting at the entrance to his tent one hot day, Abraham saw three men walking by. He hastened to greet them and urged them to rest awhile from their journey while he prepared a meal for them.

They accepted the invitation. The conversation during the meal reveals that the strangers were, in fact, God and two angels.

Hospitality is no less necessary for survival today than in Abraham's day. The deserts we traverse today are emotional and spiritual rather than physical, but survival is still the issue. Sometimes we need hospitality to survive the rigors of traveling in a spiritual desert.

The space into which I invite the weary spiritual traveler may be my home, but it is more apt to be my heart. I can offer a friend the hospitality of my heart for a few minutes over a cup of coffee, or while driving to a shopping center together. The ministry of hospitality that I received from Bill took place in a home over a period of several weeks. He welcomed me into both his home and his heart.

The ministry of spiritual hospitality grants freedom to the guest. As host, I do not demand that my guest live up to my image of what she should be. I do not require her to fill for me the roles she normally fills in daily life. Nor does she need to pretend to be something other than who she is at this moment. She does not need to wear a mask for my benefit. I allow her be who she really is.

Bill and his family did not require that I be a wise and holy priest who had it all together. They did not ask me to offer Mass for them, hear their confession or counsel them on spiritual matters. They gave me the precious freedom to be, for the moment, a weary and uncertain spiritual traveler.

Hospitality also means that I don't insist that a guest do the things that I like to do, or to do the things I think would be good for her. And I must let her determine how much togetherness or solitude she wants.

It is hard to give another this much freedom. When you find it hard to allow the person to be who she is, I suggest you concentrate on *enjoying* the person. Look at her with new eyes. Concentrate on her strengths, attributes and gifts and look for ways to affirm these.

The ministry of hospitality can be especially helpful to children. Most of us can remember some adult other than our parents to whom we could turn in time of difficulty. It may have

been a favorite aunt or a grandparent, or perhaps a neighbor.
In my neighborhood, Mrs. Herley, a widow, had this special gift
of hospitality for children. We knew we could knock at her door
anytime and we'd be welcomed. Most of our visits were casual,
but these prepared the way for serious visits in times of confusion
and crises. We could ask her questions about religion, or tell her
our worries about sex, or our troubles at school.

Once, a neighborhood family was going through a divorce.
The father had left the home. The mother was beside herself in
trying to cope, and couldn't give her children the attention they
needed. One of the children, Hilda, was six. Mrs. Herley noticed Hilda's distress and let her know she could come and visit
whenever she wanted to. Hilda later wrote me as an adult and
described her experience this way:

> Mrs. Herley saved my life. I was so upset about the
> breakup of the family. Mom was no help. I was angry
> at Dad for leaving home, but I felt guilty, too. I
> thought maybe he wouldn't have left if I'd been better.
> Mom worried about money so much that I was afraid we
> might starve. When things got too bad, I would visit
> Mrs. Herley. She would show me how to bake cookies,
> or let me help her clean house. Sometimes she helped
> me with homework lessons. I stayed overnight some-
> times. Only a few times did I tell her what was trou-
> bling me, but she seemed to know what I was going
> through anyway. I don't know what would have hap-
> pened to me without her.

Hospitality can require considerable self-sacrifice on the
part of the minister. Frequently the minister can see the deeper
need of her guest and knows that she could help, but the guest is
not open to deeper ministry. This can be frustrating. At times
like this, we must respect the person's decision, know that God's
timing is not the same as ours, and value hospitality as a ministry
in its own right—not merely as a means to deeper ministry. The
ministry of hospitality may prepare the way for a deeper kind of
helping relationship, especially with children who need to feel

very safe with the minister before they will entrust themselves to him.

When you are a minister of hospitality, be satisfied if nothing beyond hospitality happens. It is a blessing to give a time of rest and refreshment to a weary traveler. Like Abraham, you might find that unknowingly you have entertained God!

Giving Comfort

Comforting is an important, yet seldom talked-about, ministry. As a ministry, comfort flows out of a relationship characterized by *compassion*. Compassion, a God-given virtue, enables us to feel the distress of another as our own distress. It is, perhaps, the most Christ-like of all virtues. A constant refrain in the Gospels is "Jesus was moved with compassion." Jesus takes pains to make certain that we understand that this is the Father's attitude toward all human misfortune. Theologian Edward Schillebeeckz says "Showing mercy is, despite everything, the deepest purpose that God intends to fulfill in history."

Many situations today call for comfort: a person struggling with economic failure or loss of a job, the death or illness of a loved one, chronic pain or disability, disappointment with a loved one. In these situations the hurting one needs to draw upon the spiritual strength of someone who will stand with them in their suffering.

For example, a woman named Maria had a daughter, Tina, who became seriously ill at the age of two. The doctor told her that Tina had leukemia and that there was no hope for her. "Those were the worst days of my life," said Maria. "Tina cried or whimpered almost all the time, and all I could do was rock her. I had to neglect the three older kids, and they started acting up to get my attention. My husband couldn't face the fact that Tina was dying. He accused me of spoiling her and wanted me to take better care of the house. I almost went crazy."

Maria's parish had a prayer group who called themselves Healing Waters. One evening some of them came to the house and asked to "pray over" Tina. They said that if the parents just had faith, Tina would be healed. At this, Maria's husband got furious and ordered them out of the house, shouting, "Leave us alone!"

The next day, one of them phoned. "She gave me a bad time for not having enough faith," Maria said later. "She said if Tina died it would be *my* fault. I felt so guilty, but my husband was so angry with them that I just couldn't let them come."

Awhile later, another prayer group member, named Laura, phoned to ask if Maria could use some help around the house. Laura said she wouldn't pray; she'd just help. Hesitantly Maria agreed. Laura came every day for about an hour. Usually she just held Tina so that Maria could rest for an hour or catch up on housework or do something with the other children. Once or twice she talked to Laura about how helpless she felt.

Later, Maria said to me, "I guess Laura saved me from losing my mind. She was such a comfort to me." When I asked her what she had appreciated most about Laura's help. Maria said, "She just let us be, and let us work things out in our own way. She didn't give me any advice. But the best thing about her was she was just there, every day. And she could hurt, too. Sometimes she would have tears in her eyes when she was holding Tina. I could tell she cared."

The source of Laura's ministry to Maria was compassion. She eased Maria's pain by her willingness to feel it as her own pain. Comforting is a difficult ministry for twentieth century Americans. We are a "doing" people and we want immediate solutions. When no immediate solutions appear, we feel helpless, a feeling not many of us can endure for long.

The Healing Waters prayer team felt helpless when they were not permitted to help in the only way they could think of: praying for healing. Unable to tolerate feeling helpless, they blamed Maria for these feelings and gave her an additional problem of feeling guilty. Only Laura let go of the "quick fix" solution and thought of an alternative way to help. It turned out to be the way of Mary and the Beloved Disciple standing at the foot of the cross: suffering because they were not able to change things for Jesus, but comforting him by their loving presence.

Often the ministry of comforting is one of presence. An arm round the shoulders, holding someone's hand, can convey our presence to another. Listening silently without distraction is another way. Sometimes reading Scripture gives comfort, but it must not be used to avoid sharing the person's pain.

Laura had the courage to offer comfort. To feel Maria's—and Tina's—pain required considerable courage. It is no wonder that we frequently attempt to avoid entering into the person's pain by saying such things as: "Everything will be all right," or "God will not forget you," or "Praise God anyway." Laura had the courage to listen to Maria's pain without cutting her off with hollow reassurances or pious platitudes.

Accepting Self-Disclosure

Matthew, a colleague of mine, tells this story when he teaches about accepting self-disclosure. One day his niece, Jean, dropped by and asked if she could talk to him about an important matter. He invited her in, and she began by saying, "I have this huge logjam blocking me from God. I can't budge it, I can't climb over it and I can't get around it. I need help."

Matthew asked Jean when her "logjam" began, and she responded by saying she had done "something terrible" that she couldn't stand to think about. She sat opposite Matthew with her hands clasped tightly in her lap. Matthew gently asked, "Can you tell me what it is? Maybe I can help."

"Well," she answered, not looking him, "I was having a lot of trouble with Mom and didn't know what to do. I went to a favorite teacher of mine from last year and talked to him about it. He listened to me and then made some suggestions that were so neat I felt like a new person. I wanted him to know how grateful I was, so I thanked him and then I threw my arms around his neck and kissed him! And he's a married man! I feel so guilty I could die! I went to confession and the priest said it wasn't a sin, but I still feel guilty. I used to stop by and visit that teacher sometimes, but now I can't go near his room. I blew it."

Matthew told me that he encouraged Jean to talk more about her feelings of guilt by acknowledging them as her genuine feelings. He told her he knew they were painful to her. The discussion that followed enabled her to see her actions in a new light. She was able to see she had not intended to dishonor the teacher's commitment to his wife, but to express gratitude to him. She also decided that her expression of gratitude, while not appropriate, was understandable as girlish enthusiasm. Then Matthew prayed with her that she might accept the Father's love for her.

Matthew ended his story by saying that some weeks later Jean called him and said, "Your prayers worked, Uncle. That log-jam is gone. Besides that, I went back and talked to the teacher and it's O.K. now."

Matthew gave Jean a great gift. This is a ministry close to the heart of Jesus. He practiced it often. Think of Jesus accept-ing the outpouring of Mary Magdalene's sorrow when she anointed his feet during a dinner party. We know how this freed her to change her sinful way of life and become the saint God had always intended. Now that he has ascended to the Father, Jesus expects us to continue this ministry. Matthew's listening seriously to Jean's feelings about the "terrible thing" she had done freed her to continue her spiritual journey and to grow into the kind of person God intended.

Matthew's situation shows us how important it is to accept the person's definition of the problem and his or her feelings about it. By telling Jean he heard her pain and by accepting her feelings, Matthew enabled her to see her actions through God's eyes. This freed Jean from guilt and enabled her to once again be friends with God and with her teacher. The logjam was bro-ken.

The priest who heard Jean's confession did not accept her definition of her problem. He dismissed her concern by saying she had not sinned. But this was not her basic issue, which was one of shame. She needed someone to be with her as she ex-plored an embarrassing moment in her life. In her present state of mind, she did not need to learn about the theology of sin.

Our deep respect for supplicants will free them to bring into the light those experiences of life that they judge most shameful. This will enable them to rid themselves of their shame and see themselves in a new way. Sometimes they come to us with a mistaken opinion about the meaning of their actions (as Jean did). Ultimately we will need to correct that and help them accept God's outlook. But this is a *goal* in healing ministry. Accepting self-disclosure means we start where the supplicant is, at that point in time.

One important caution: Often we can see things about a person that are hidden from him. It is a mistake to uncover deeper reasons for a problem until the person is ready! Jean's anxiety about kissing her teacher may have been a symptom of unresolved conflicts about her sexuality. But she was not ready to look at that. It would have been a mistake for Matthew to have raised that issue.

Instruction

One night at a prayer meeting, a girl named Rita prayed: "Oh God, give me the courage to go job-hunting. Please help me. I am so afraid!" The group, with some embarrassment, murmured, "Lord, hear this prayer."

Rita was an awkward, immature adolescent who was about to graduate from high school. Her parents were divorced. She lived with her father, who suffered from alcoholism. Her mother lived in a distant city. Rita felt frightened and confused by the prospect of supporting herself.

When the prayer meeting ended, Marion, an experienced legal secretary, approached Rita and offered to coach her as she prepared to enter the job market. Rita eagerly accepted the offer. In the following weeks, Marion taught her how to dress and use makeup, what to say during a job interview, how to behave in an office, and how to relate to other employees. The prayer group marveled to see this gawky, inept girl blossom into a responsible woman over a period of just a few months.

Marion was ministering "instruction" to Rita. She gave her the precise information needed at this stage of her life's journey. One way to describe the ministry of instruction is to tell what it is *not*:

- It is not classroom teaching, which imparts information to students in a systematic and general way for their future use. Classroom teaching can be a valuable ministry, but is not the ministry of instruction.
- It is not unsolicited advice-giving, which runs rampant in religious circles and is totally useless. Most advice-giving overflows with "oughts" and "shoulds," which the hearer already knows.

Three principles govern the effectiveness of instruction:

- First, it must flow out of a special relationship which is important to the person receiving the ministry. This "specialness" existed between Marion and Rita. Marion was a mature, successful working woman whom Rita could look up to, especially since both shared similar religious values. They had known each other for some time in the prayer group and had common friends and experiences there. Marion saw potential in Rita and liked her. She wanted to help her grow into that potential. Marion had the information and experience that Rita needed at that moment. No one else in Rita's life at that moment could have done for her what Marion did. Often there will be more than one person who can minister instruction effectively, but it cannot be just anyone.
- The second principle for effective instruction is that it can only be given at teachable moments in a person's life. There are critical stages in our lives when we are especially open to receive and to make use of instruction in ways that will bring healing or growth. A psychological readiness exists during each stage (which may endure over many months or even years). In Rita's case, the same instruction given a year earlier would not have been helpful to her. Marion's coaching was usable to Rita only when she was experiencing anxiety about her future. Before then, it would have been unsolicited advice giving.
- The third factor governing the effectiveness of instruction is that a struggle usually exists to incorporate the new information into one's way of thinking. The struggle was minor with

Rita, but often changing an old habit or thought process involves great effort.

For example, I recall Philip, a middle-aged Catholic, who came to see me because a friend had suggested to him that I might be able to help him with his "problem about Holy Communion."

Philip told me he was nervous because he had never talked to a priest like this before. When I responded that it must be hard to talk about his problem to me, he agreed, but said it also was a relief.

Ten years earlier, Philip's wife had divorced him. He didn't want the divorce and never remarried. He said, "I knew that when you get a divorce you are automatically excommunicated and are forbidden to receive Holy Communion. I was telling my friend how bad I feel about never being able to receive Holy Communion again and he said I should talk to you."

I informed Philip he had misunderstood the teaching of the Catholic church. Excommunication was attached to remarriage when one was still validly married according to church law, even though divorced by civil law. It was not attached to the divorce itself.

Philip had some trouble understanding what I was saying, so we discussed it in some detail. When he fully understood me, he said: "Are you a liberal or conservative?" He was afraid that I was not presenting the "real" teaching of the church, but instead a lax personal opinion. In response, I showed him the law as written in a book on church law. I thought he would be overjoyed at this, but he wasn't. It was so different from what he had believed for so long that he was shaken. Finally he said, "I don't know; can I come back after I think it over?"

When Philip returned the following week he said, "It's hard to think about this in a new way, but it would be worse for pride to keep me from receiving Our Lord. And I really do want to go to Holy Communion." I heard his Confession and he received Holy Communion at a private Mass I celebrated with his close friend present. Philip was overcome with joy at being able to receive communion once again. He said to his friend and me,

"You two have given me the best gift I've ever received. Thank you!"

The teachable moment means that there is an urge to move ahead. But at the same time, there is pain in giving up old ways of thinking and acting. The minister of instruction needs to be prepared for a recipient's struggle to accept new information. Otherwise she might be offended by behavior such as Philip showed toward me on our first meeting. Helping the supplicant to accept the information is part of the ministry.

The ministry of instruction deserves to be more highly valued. It is an important way of helping others. Jesus spent a great deal of time instructing the twelve apostles. The time and care he gave to instructing them bore fruit: it changed their lives and they, in turn, changed the course of the world's history.

Jesus continues this ministry of instruction through us as members of His Body. I urge ministers of healing prayer to be alert to opportunities to give this kind of help when it is sought. It is not necessary that we have all the information personally, as Marion did. Our job may be to refer the person to someone who is more knowledgeable on a topic, as Philip's friend did for him. We may give someone a book or a pamphlet; we may accompany someone to an agency or to a resource person. But however we impart the information, it must be tailored to the person's situation, it must flow out of a special relationship with the person, and it must be given at a teachable moment.

For Further Reading

1. *Helping When It Hurts,* by Robert L. Hunter. Fortress Press, 1985.

Summary—Chapter 12

This chapter describes four traditional Christian ministries that often go unrecognized, but which are powerful tools for healing:

1. Extending hospitality.

A. In the ministry of hospitality, we invite the weary spiritual traveler into our personal space. Sometimes it's our home. More often it's our heart.

B. The ministry of spiritual hospitality grants freedom to the guest to be who he really is. This can happen by focusing on the enjoyment of the strengths and attributes of the guest.

2. Giving comfort.

A. As a ministry, comfort flows out of compassion, which enables us to feel the distress of another as our own distress.

B. Often the ministry of comforting is one of presence, e.g., an arm around the shoulders, attentively listening.

3. Accepting self-disclosure.

Our profound reverence for the validity of people's feelings enables them to disclose deeds they are ashamed of. We then can help them allow God's love to heal them of that shame.

4. Instruction.

A. This is not classroom teaching or unsolicited advice.

B. Three principles govern the effectiveness of instruction:

  1. It flows out of a special relationship which is important to the person receiving the ministry.

  2. It can only be given at teachable moments.

  3. A struggle usually exists to incorporate the new information into one's way of thinking.

For Your Reflection—Chapter 12

1. Review the chapter summary, which lists four traditional ministries that often go unrecognized. How many of these have you used to offer help to someone in need? Which one have you used the most? the least? At the time you used them, did you recognize them as ministry? (cf. Mt 25:35-40)

2. Think of an occasion when you were helped by someone using one of these unrecognized ministries. What did he or she do? At the time, did you see this as God bringing healing into your life through this person's efforts? If it's appropriate, consider writing this person a letter, thanking them for what they did for you in that situation. If that isn't possible, then write a letter to Jesus, thanking him for sending this person into your life just when you needed help.

3. 2 Cor 1:3-4 (TEV) says, "Let us give thanks to the God and Father of our Lord Jesus Christ, the merciful Father, the God from whom all help comes! He helps us in all our troubles, so that we are able to help others who have all kinds of troubles, using the same help that we ourselves have received from God." Reflect on the specific ways God has helped you in your troubles by sending people to minister to you. Then ask yourself how the help that you have received can enable you to reach out to others who are in trouble. In what ways can you pass on these helps to others?

13

The Minister of Religious Healing[1]

❖   ❖   ❖   ❖   ❖

The woman on the other end of the phone identified herself as Lila and announced to me that God had given her a healing ministry. She also informed me that she wanted to work with me in ministry.

This was not the first time I had received a call like this, so I knew what Lila expected of me. She expected me to rejoice with a "Praise the Lord!" But I felt deeply suspicious and did not want to be falsely encouraging. Weakly, I replied that I directed a two-year program of training for healing ministry and would be glad to send her a flyer describing the program.

"Father," she said, "you don't understand. When I was Baptized in the Holy Spirit, I received the gift of healing. *God* has given me this ministry. I don't need training." I, in turn, said that God might indeed have given her the gift of healing, but the Christian Community needs to discern the authenticity of any ministry gift and has the responsibility to offer training so that Christians can develop their gifts. This takes time. At this, Lila accused me of being unspiritual, called me a godless, secular humanist, and slammed down the receiver.

---

1. Author's note: Chapter 2 of *Healing as a Parish Ministry* describes the following woman in detail. Of all the people I've met, she best illustrates what the above book calls a "Jesus-and-me" spirituality.

From previous experience, I knew what probably would happen next. Lila would launch out with a "lone ranger" ministry, grind up a number of vulnerable, hurting souls who accepted her ministry, alienate several clergy and discredit the ministry of religious healing. In the end, she would become embittered and withdraw from the institutional church.

I believe that God calls people to the ministry of religious healing, and I believe that God bestows gifts of healing upon the Body of Christ. But even someone so dramatically called as St. Paul spent three years in Arabia, presumably readying himself for ministry by prayer and study. He started his ministry not as a "Lone Ranger," but when he was called to it by the Christian Community at Antioch through the person of Barnabas. All major Christian denominations require a long period of training and demonstrated competence before they ordain their ministers.

People like Lila may develop into ministers of religious healing *if* they are humble enough to take the time to discern and to develop their gifts. But their pride and impatience often deprives the Body of Christ of a meaningful ministry.

Another type of person also deprives the Body of Christ of healing ministry. These are the souls so timid that it never even occurs to them that God might call them to any kind of ministry. If someone brings this to their attention, they excuse themselves by saying they are not worthy to be used by God. Their inadequate response to God's call is seldom noticed.

For instance, Corinne was an unassuming but friendly woman who for years had taken care of the altar linen in her parish, prepared the altar for Mass each day and often spent time praying before the Blessed Sacrament. I served in the same parish and noticed how Corinne's attentiveness to visitors and newcomers would cause them to brighten up. She impressed me as a mature Christian with potential as a minister of healing. Therefore I asked her to consider taking part in our training program.

She expressed surprise and anxiety, telling me she could never pray aloud for people. I said maybe not, but added that I thought she might discover some new gifts within herself. After considerable inner struggle, Corinne did enroll in the first year of the program.

At the end of the year, she said it had been a time of spiritual growth for her. Her teachers reported that everyone valued her quiet wisdom and genial personality. Yet Corinne hesitated about entering the second year of the program because it would mean she would be on a prayer team, praying for supplicants. Finally she relented. Supplicants responded well to her nurturing personality and her compassion for their pain.

Corinne moved forward on her journey as a minister of religious healing, yet she trembled at every new step. When I asked her to be a team leader in the training program, she said she felt too scared to do that. Finally, however, she agreed. When she graduated from the program and I suggested she contact her pastor to discuss forming healing ministry in the parish, she balked, then ultimately consented. Corinne's team has been functioning now for several years. Their pastor sees their ministry as a valuable resource for the parish.

Except for her lack of self-confidence, Corinne had all the qualities needed to be an excellent healing minister. She is representative of many people's lack of awareness of their gifts. Only slowly, with the help of others, did she recognize them and become willing to put them at the service of the Body of Christ.

People sometimes associate the opposite, Lila-type person with the Charismatic Renewal Movement. Its spirituality provides a powerful experience of the release of the power of the Holy Spirit in people's lives. The event is called by a variety of names: Baptism in the Holy Spirit, Release of the Holy Spirit and Pentecostal Experience. Lila had this experience, and gifts of healing may have been released in her at that time.

But spiritual power, like all other forms of power, can be used well or badly. The gifts associated with the ministry of religious healing are especially prone to these destructive uses. Many people feel tempted to use them to bolster their own egos by gaining the recognition of others as a special person, or by exercising control over people's lives in God's name.

No matter how powerful a gift of healing may be, ministers of religious healing need a long period of using the traditional

Christian disciplines of prayer, study and accountability to enable them to use their spiritual gifts constructively. Unfortunately some balk at undergoing the discipline of learning how to use God's gift for the good of others. Some refuse to discipline their own needs so that they don't get in the way.

Many make another mistake by focusing exclusively on the charism of healing. They refuse to value and develop both their natural gifts and God-given virtues such as faith, love, prudence and fortitude. This is a mistake because the effective use of the charisms of the Holy Spirit must build upon one's natural gifts and virtues.[2] It is a tragedy when someone squanders the gifts God offers through her to the Christian Community.

Corinne almost squandered God's gift of healing by not paying attention to and developing it. Her timidity blinded her from seeing the gifts God had given her. However, eventually she heeded God's call because she had learned the Christian disciplines of regular prayer and quiet service to others.

Qualities of a Healing Minister

Although God uses all kinds of unlikely people to do His work, a core of qualities seems to be needed to be an effective minister of religious healing. I think the nucleus of this core is the ability to lead a supplicant into an experience of Jesus meeting her in her need. From this flow several other core qualities, which differ according to the culture and personality of the supplicant. No one person can lead everyone into an experience of Jesus. But four qualities ministers need are:

1. a lively, vivid, personal relationship with Jesus. This needs to have matured through the practice of the traditional christian disciplines;

2. the ability to listen deeply to the supplicant;

3. a motivation for ministry that is based on compassion;

4. the knowledge and skill to put this compassion to work to heal the wounds the supplicant has presented.

---

2. Chapter 18 goes into detail about all of God's gifts.

Training for Healing Ministry

What exists today

Ideally, every diocese would offer in-depth training programs for ministers of religious healing. Those people who felt called by God to this ministry could attend a program within their geographic area. Upon completion of the program, and with the discernment by others of their call, they would take their gifts, knowledge and experience back into their parishes, where they would offer God's tender healing to hurting parishioners.

Unfortunately, a gap often exists between the real and the ideal. Nowhere is the gap wider than in the availability of solid training programs offered to potential ministers of religious healing. I discuss this topic knowing that in today's church, many dedicated Christians seek what they cannot find: a way to develop their God-given gifts of healing.

However, some programs do exist. Those who want to become ministers of religious healing now have several choices:

1. They can attend an on-site, intensive training program. But few can afford the time and money it takes to leave home and live elsewhere while taking an on-site course.

2. They can attend an in-depth program that teaches broad pastoral-care skills. But most of these programs do not teach their students how to do *prayer* ministry, which is a major need in today's world.

3. They can attend programs that teach healing ministry in a day, a weekend or a few evenings. Short programs can introduce people to healing ministry or upgrade certain skills for specific problems, such as how to minister to the dying. Unfortunately, some newcomers presume that after 5 or 10 hours they are fully ready to be "healers." Spiritual maturity cannot be achieved in a few hours. Nor can competency be reached in such a short time.

4. People can listen to audiotapes on healing. But most of these tapes exist for the purpose of *self* help. Rather than

training people for ministry, they foster each listener's personal growth and healing.

5. They can take an in-depth program over an extended period of time that offers spiritual formation and teaches "how-to" skills. This is what I developed in conjunction with several other professionals. But as with the first option (the on-site, intensive program), our Institute for Christian Ministries is only available in several places. We are creating a teaching packet for others to use in developing their own program, but it is difficult to pass on wisdom, experience and spiritual formation without personal interactions between students and teachers.

With the reality of today's scarcity of programs in mind, I offer the following suggestions for the goals I think a good training program should strive to achieve.

Goals for training in healing ministry

Goal #1: to foster spiritual maturity through a process of spiritual formation. Watching the healing ministry of a spiritually immature Christian is like being present at dismissal time at a high school. In the latter scene, invariably one sees a few childish students with new driver's licenses. Awed by their new-found power, they zoom around heedless of anyone else. They risk everyone's well-being by their misuse of power. So too, an immature minister of religious healing gets so caught up with himself and his gifts that he loses sight of the supplicant and even of God.

Through the misuse of power, healing ministers can cause great harm to others. Therefore, *I believe that any training program for the ministry of religious healing should make spiritual formation its primary goal.*

Spiritual formation moves Christians from immaturity to maturity. Along the journey, their knowledge of God and of themselves grows. God becomes real to them in a life-changing, experiential way. Mature ministers have the ability to enable their supplicants to experience God at a deep, healing level. Since a primary goal of healing ministry is to make God present to the supplicant, this can only be achieved through ministers to whom God is already profoundly present. Arising from a faith-filled relationship with Christ, a minister's natural and supernatural gifts can be used in a way that heals instead of harms.

Goal #2: to teach the knowledge, skills and attitudes needed for successful ministry. No one can become a physician after a weekend first-aid course. And no one can become a competent minister of religious healing after only a few hours of study. Why? Because healing ministers need knowledge and many skills, none of which comes with a ZAP from God. The knowledge must include an awareness of and a respect for medical and psychological wisdom.

Healing ministers need good teachers and an affirming learning environment. Through this, they discover and learn how to use many gifts, both natural and supernatural. In the Institute for Christian Ministries, one learning tool we use is extensive reading assignments. This book and *Born to Win* include self-reflection exercises, which help students connect newly-acquired knowledge with their past, lived experiences.

Goal #3: to teach team healing ministry. Personally, I believe that team healing ministry is the ideal way to minister healing to hurting supplicants. No one person possesses all the natural and supernatural gifts needed in this ministry. When people work together on a team, their gifts, knowledge and skills combine to create a ministry that is far more powerful and effective than that of a soloist. Also, in team ministry, one person's mistakes are less likely to do harm. For these reasons, I encourage healing teams as the preferred method of ministry. Trainees need to be taught how to work together on a prayer team, since team unity is critical to the success of team ministry.

Goal #4: to help each trainee determine to what extent he is called to this ministry. Program leaders should not assume that God is calling each of their trainees into healing ministry. Dysfunctional people sometimes seek to enter this ministry as a way to solve their own problems. And not all psychologically healthy people are called to formal healing ministry. Even though God calls every Christian to some ministry, no individual possesses the unique characteristics needed for every ministry. As has been true for the past 2,000 years, church leaders bear the responsibility of discerning ministerial gifts. This responsibility includes discovering and affirming people's gifts within the ministry of religious healing.

This ministry serves as a support for many fields (spiritual, medical, and psychological). Therefore, trainees need help in discovering their particular gifts beneath the overall umbrella of healing ministry. They need help in discerning in what specific area God is calling them to use these gifts.

Future training programs in healing ministry

I believe that the ministry of religious healing is coming back into the mainstream of the Church. After centuries of relative neglect, Jesus' command to "cure the sick, raise the dead, cleanse lepers, cast out devils" (JB, Mt 10:8a) is being heard by many as a call to bring healing ministry into everyday parish life. For this to happen effectively, Church leaders will need to offer quality training programs in every diocese.

If those who feel called by God into this ministry gently yet persistently make their needs known to their pastors and other leaders, I believe that future training programs will blossom. Jesus' vision of people having the fullness of life will become a reality throughout the world.

For Further Reading

1. *Ministry: A Theological, Pastoral Handbook,* by Richard McBrien. Harper and Row, 1987.

2. *Experiencing Jesus,* by John Wijngaards. Ave Maria Press, 1981.

3. *Born to Win,* by Muriel James and Dorothy Jongeward. Addison-Wesley Publishing, 1971.

Summary—Chapter 13

A. God calls people to the ministry of religious healing and bestows gifts of healing upon the Body of Christ. Those called can deprive the Body of Christ of healing ministry in two ways:

1. They can become "lone rangers," refusing to take the time to discern and develop their gift. Incompetence and misuse of spiritual power harms the ministry of religious healing.

2. They can deny God's call through over-timidity, regarding themselves as unworthy to be used by God.

B. Ministers of religious healing need several core qualities:

1. a personal relationship with Jesus that has matured through the practice of traditional christian disciplines;

2. the ability to listen deeply;

3. a motivation for ministry that is based on compassion;

4. the knowledge and skill to put this compassion to work.

C. Training for team ministry requires much time and effort on the part of students and teachers. Goals should include:

1. Fostering spiritual maturity through a process of spiritual formation. This should be the primary goal for any training program.

2. Teaching the knowledge, skills and attitudes needed for successful ministry.

3. Teaching team healing ministry.

4. Helping each trainee determine to what extent he is called to this ministry.

For Your Reflection—Chapter 13

1. To help you consider the ministry of religious healing for yourself, look at the chapter summary to review the four core qualities needed for effective ministers. On a scale of 1 to 10, how would you rate yourself for each of qualities? What would you need to do to develop these qualities sufficiently to be an effective minister of religious healing?

2. The prophets would have understood Corinne's reluctance to answer God's call to healing ministry. Read Jer 1:4-10, then picture yourself in Jeremiah's place, being called by God but arguing about the call. Jeremiah used the excuse that he didn't know how to speak; he was "too young" (vs. 6). If you've ever resisted God's call to engage in ministry, what argument did *you* use? Envision yourself placing that argument before Jesus, then ask him to give you the grace to say "yes" to whatever ministry he has in mind for you.

3. Take some time to examine what options for training for healing ministry exist within your community, e.g., parish training for bringing communion to shut-ins? a hospital training program for volunteer pastoral care workers? a Stephen Series? a hospice training program? books and/or a videotape series? Which of these training options might be possible for you? If there is any cost involved, what options exist for financing your training? Ask God to show you His will for you as regards training for this ministry.

Part II

Spiritual Resources for Ministers of Religious Healing

May (God) enlighten your inmost vision that you may
know . . . the immeasurable scope of his power in us
who believe. It is like the strength he showed in raising
Jesus from the dead. (NAB, Eph 1:18-20)

This prayer of Paul's says that Christians have resurrection
power! Am I to believe this? If so, Paul is right in praying that we
grasp the scope of the power working through us. Our minds cannot comprehend that the same power works in us that raised Jesus
from the dead. It is God's power, of course, but it works through us.

This special section describes a number of resources that are
available to us as ministers of religious healing. These resources are:

1. Prayer of Affirmation
2. Sacramentals
3. Laying on of Hands
4. Resting in the Spirit
5. Spiritual Gifts

When we use these resources in faith, God heals the hurts
of his wounded children. I join my prayer with St. Paul's that all
of us may come to know the immeasurable scope of God's power
resident in our ministry to the wounded and sorrowful members
of Christ's Body.

14

Prayer of Affirmation

❖　　　❖　　　❖　　　❖　　　❖

Many of us share a common problem of thinking we are a disappointment to everyone, especially to God. In Chapter 3, the supplicant named Larry began to sob when his team prayed a prayer of affirmation for him. For the first time in his life he experienced God's approval of him.

Our society behaves in a number of ways that destroy people's self-esteem. First, like Larry, our competitive culture concentrates upon our failures and inadequacies and points them out to us in an effort to make us do better. Parents, teachers, bosses, often criticize our performance. They push us to do better by belittling what we have done. They compare our efforts unfavorably to the accomplishments of siblings, classmates and co-workers. They mean well, but *constant criticism* tears down our self-esteem. Like Larry, we begin to see ourselves as failures and a disappointment to others.

Our culture also engages in *negative humor*, which destroys people's self-esteem. Instead of using compliments to acknowledge an achievement, people often use negative humor. This twists the compliment into a put-down. For example, if a man makes a strike in bowling, his partner may say: "Well, you finally did something right!" His achievement has become an excuse for a put-down instead of a cause for rejoicing.

Discounting is another common practice that tears down self-esteem. It diminishes a person's self-esteem to his or her face. For instance, a husband discounts his wife if he introduces her to his friends as "just a housewife," uses unflattering names for her such as "my old lady," or treats her suggestions as unworthy of serious consideration. A wife discounts her husband if, for instance, she interrupts him whenever he begins to speak. Parents discount a child if, for example, they angrily call him names when he accidentally knocks over a glass of milk and shout, "You're so clumsy! Can't you do anything right?"

This constant barrage of criticism, negative humor, and discounting so damages our self esteem that we are not able to become the person God intends. We internalize society's messages and become highly critical of ourselves; we become blind to our own goodness. From this, it's a short step to thinking that all of our self-criticism comes from others, especially from God. We find it difficult to believe that others—especially God—approve of us.

And so we begin to believe that all of the criticisms, all of the negative jokes, all of the discounting statements, are true. We come to believe the Big Lie, which says that we are of no worth. It becomes a way of life for us. The Big Lie prevents us from seeing and using the gifts that God has given us to work for His kingdom. Satan, whom Jesus called the Father of Lies, uses this deception to further his kingdom.

Thus, **the fundamental need of almost every supplicant is the healing of a wounded self-esteem.** Affirmation is an especially powerful resource given to us by God to achieve this healing. Affirmation consists of three steps.

1. See the goodness within a person as being a gift from God.

2. Allow yourself to be so moved by seeing that goodness, that you give thanks to God for the person.

3. Express that thanksgiving in some external way to the person himself. In ministry, you can do this by a direct statement or by the prayer of affirmation.

Direct positive feedback about the goodness we see in a person is affirming. Most people receive so little positive feedback and are so critical of themselves that they need help to recognize the gifts they have. You might say directly to a supplicant, "You have such a lovely gift of deep trust in God's desire to heal you. Your trust builds up my faith. Thank you."

Another way to externalize one's thankfulness for a suppliant's goodness is by a prayer of affirmation. Here the minister gives thanks directly to God for the suppliant, in the suppliant's presence. I remember the prayer of affirmation that I was moved to say for a woman names Genevieve. She was a single, working mother of five children who asked me to pray with her about her fourteen year old daughter who was being "mouthy." On one occasion, Genevieve had become furious and had slapped her. Her reaction frightened her. She herself had been a physically abused child, and she feared repeating the pattern of physical abuse.

My prayer for Genevieve went something like this: "Lord God, I give you thanks for Genevieve I thank you for the gift she is to her family. I thank you for the joy with which she takes care of her family. I thank you for the ready smile she has in times of difficulty. I thank you that you have gifted her with a heart that is open to others in their times of trial and pain. Lord, I thank you for the deep faith that Genevieve has in the healing power of your Son, Jesus. I thank you for the courage she has to step forward in faith and ask for healing."

One caution: Affirmation must not degenerate into empty flattery or trite phrases. A supplicant will sense its phoniness and this will damage her trust in the minister. Affirmation is not a technique that we can use at will. In whatever way it's given, true affirmation is a form of prayer by which we praise God for his handiwork. The prayer of affirmation, like the prayer of praise, is the work of the Holy Spirit. We cannot pray on our own power. St. Paul tells us that we cannot so much as proclaim that "Jesus is Lord" except by the power of the Holy Spirit (1 Cor 12:3). If I find myself praying the same thing about each person, or if I can't think of anything to affirm, these signs tell me I need to pray that the Holy Spirit revive in me the gift of affirmation. For this to happen, I may need to spend time in private prayer praising God for each supplicant. I must pray frequently that God's gift of affirmation will grow so strong in me that affirmation becomes my way of life.

For Further Reading

1. *Your Child's Self-Esteem,* by Dorothy Briggs. Dolphin, 1975.

Summary—Chapter 14

A. Society often damages people's self-esteem through a variety of techniques, including:

1. Constant criticism—belittling, fault-finding, etc.

2. Negative humor—apparent "humor" that's done at someone's expense

3. Discounting—statements that diminish a person's innate value as a child of God.

B. The fundamental need of almost every supplicant is the healing of a wounded self-esteem. Affirmation can help heal that wound.

C. Affirmation consists of three steps:

1. See the goodness within a person as being a gift from God.

2. Allow yourself to be so moved by seeing that goodness that you give thanks to God for the person.

3. Express that thanksgiving in some external way to the person himself, e.g. direct statement or prayer of affirmation.

D. Definition of affirmation:

1. It is *not* empty flattery or trite phrases.

2. It is *not* a technique that we use at will.

3. True affirmation, in whatever way it's given, is a form of prayer by which we praise God for his handiwork.

For Your Reflection—Chapter 14

1. Select some person close to you that you want to affirm, e.g., a spouse, child, friend. Pray briefly to the Holy Spirit, asking for guidance, then follow the chapter summary's three steps for affirming that person: *Step #1:* Jot down several good traits you see in him/her. *Step #2:* Allow yourself to be so moved by that goodness that you give thanks to God for him/her. *Step #3:* Write a note to that person, affirming the goodness you see in him/her. *If* you think it would be appropriate, give/mail the letter to the person.

2. Think of a time when someone affirmed you in some important way. How did that affirmation affect your spiritual life?

3. Nearly all of St. Paul's letters/epistles begin with affirmation of the recipients. Reflect on one or two of the following passages by imagining that St. Paul is talking directly to *you:* Rm 1:8; 1 Cor 1:4-7; Eph 1:15-16; Phil 1:3-5; Col 1:3-5; 1 Thes 1:2-3, 6-9; 2 Thes 1:3-4. How do you feel? Can you allow yourself to believe that St. Paul is addressing you? If this is difficult, spend a few minutes in prayer, asking Jesus for the grace to receive the affirmation of others, including St. Paul.

15

Sacramentals

❖   ❖   ❖   ❖   ❖

Sacramentals are a valuable resource for ministers of religious healing. Those most frequently used are holy water, blessed oil, salt, candles, the cross, banners and flowers. Through our use of these fruits of creation, God makes real to us his presence, beauty, and power. A correct understanding of sacramentals helps the minister use them effectively.

The prototype for all sacramentals is the Incarnation—the Word made flesh. When God decided to become present to his people in a new and unique way—through the Son taking on human nature—something totally new happened. The invisible and intangible reality of God became known to us through the visible human life of Jesus of Nazareth. Jesus himself put it in its simplest terms when he said: "Whoever has seen me has seen the Father." (TEV, Jn 14:9)

But Jesus, knowing that he was going to ascend to the Father after his death and resurrection, was concerned about future generations who would not see him in the flesh. So he gave us the Sacraments. Their use by the Christian community continues Christ's presence among us and imparts a share of his divine life to us. Ordinarily, the sacraments are administered only by an ordained minister when the Christian community is gathered in an official way: for example, the Eucharist celebrated in church on Sunday.

Christians often need symbols in everyday life to remind them of the continued presence and power of Christ. So over the centuries, the Christian community has followed the example of Jesus and made use of symbols in addition to the sacraments. These we call sacramentals. They are articles of everyday use— water, oil, salt, candles—made holy by the prayer of the Christian community, i.e., they are blessed. Used "in faith," these blessed articles make Christ's presence and power more real in our everyday life.

Magical thinking about sacramentals is a real danger, but clarity about their true meaning helps us use this resource correctly. We use them "in faith," faith in God's benevolence and power. We do not believe that sacramentals possess a power in themselves with which we can control our environment. That belief would place us in the realm of practicing magic. Instead, sacramentals are intended to stimulate our faith in Christ's power. For example, when I light a blessed candle as a holy symbol, I am reminded that Christ is present as the light of the world, and that it is he who overcomes the darkness.

We bring faith to the use of sacramentals, but their use stirs us to even greater faith. For example, when I bless myself or others with holy water, I am reminded that I have been baptized into Christ and am a well-loved child of God.

Ministers of religious healing sometimes ask how to know which sacramental to use. The question betrays a wrong understanding of sacramentals. They differ from a doctor's prescription of medicine for a certain ailment. Each medicine has a particular effect: it changes the chemistry of the body in a special way. Sacramentals work differently. They work by way of symbolism. Their use is guided by the way a particular symbol affects a particular supplicant. The proper question to ask is, "Will this sacramental help this supplicant experience Christ as present to him in love and with power to meet his need?"

Admittedly this is not a simple guideline. It's difficult to know what meaning a certain sacramental will have for which supplicant. Another difficulty is that each sacramental symbolizes many different things. Water, for example, symbolizes God's gift of divine life because water is the source of all life. But because it also is a natural cleansing agent, it symbolizes the forgiveness of sin. And on the natural level, water symbolizes refreshment—when weary, we take a leisurely shower or hot bath.

Therefore, water can carry the meaning of the Holy Spirit refreshing us in times of spiritual weariness.

Here are four sacramentals that may be helpful to you:

1. Blessed water

Blessed water's many symbolic meanings make this sacramental a powerful aid in the ministry of healing. For example,
bathing the head of a person who is physically sick and weak is a
sign of Jesus giving them more of his Abundant Life. Blessed
water carries the meaning of refreshment for a supplicant who is
weary from a long struggle with drug addiction. As you bless
him with holy water, its meaning can be strengthen by reading
the words of Jesus "Come to me all of you who are tired from
carrying heavy loads and I will refresh you . . ." (TEV, Mt 11:28)

Many ministers find it helpful to bless the whole team as
they prepare for ministry. It reminds them that they have been
baptized in Christ and are gathering as his people to minister in
his Name. When ministry is especially difficult, it helps to use
holy water to make the sign of the cross upon the ministers &/or
the supplicant. This gesture reminds everyone that by his cross
and resurrection, Jesus has won the victory over all evil. Sometimes during ministry the team experiences an especially intense
activity of evil spirits attempting to hinder the ministry. When
this occurs, it's helpful to sprinkle the area and the people as a
reminder that Jesus has defeated Satan.

The symbolism of water as a cleansing agent helped greatly
in ministering to a woman who had been sexually assaulted. She
could not get free of feeling violated. As she expressed it, "I feel
dirty and damaged." Sex, for her, had become so confused with
violence that even sex with her loving husband tormented her. I
suggested she draw a tub of warm water, pour in a bottle of holy
water which I gave her, and soak in it as she prayed. I instructed
her how to use imagery in prayer. We discussed the kind of images she felt comfortable in using. She chose to imagine herself
as an infant being bathed tenderly by Mary, with Jesus, as her
older brother, present. She visualized Jesus' cleansing, healing
power being present in the bath water. She did this every day for

a week. She reported it contributed to remarkable progress in being healed of the destructive feelings about herself and about sex.

2. Blessed oil

The official book of blessing prayers for the Roman Catholic church contains a blessing for oil to be used by the laity. It is this oil that I am speaking of here, *not* the oil blessed by a bishop (or, in some special circumstances by a priest) to be used in administering the Sacrament of Anointing of the Sick. In Roman Catholic thought, a clear distinction between the two blessings is important because the administration of the Sacrament of Anointing the Sick is reserved to an ordained priest, and the oil blessed for that sacrament must not to be used by a non-ordained minister. *Catholic lay ministers must take care that, in using oil blessed for lay use, the recipient of ministry does not think he has received the Sacrament of the Anointing of the Sick.* Roman Catholic bishops and priests are rightly concerned about confusion regarding its official Sacraments.

But with that caution in mind, the use of blessed oil plays an important role in the ministry of religious healing. Oil carries two symbolic meanings in ministry: healing and consecration.

In biblical times, people used oil to heal wounds. Even today, oil is used in lotions for the massage of aching muscles and for the prevention of bedsores in hospitals patients. The symbolism of oil, as a soothing and healing agent, makes it useful in the ministry of prayer for physical healing. The minister can rub it on or near the afflicted part of the body if that can be decently done. Or the supplicant himself can do so. Otherwise it may be applied to the forehead as standing for the whole person. The application is accompanied with a prayer for healing that will stir up faith that God will use this sacramental as a means of healing. A good practice is to give the supplicant a small bottle of oil to use as she continues to pray for healing at home.

Blessed oil also may be used in ministering to emotional, spiritual or relational wounds. In ministering to someone who is brokenhearted, I ask her to anoint herself over her heart while I pray that the Lord heal her brokenness. In praying for healing of memories, I anoint the supplicant's forehead.

In biblical times, oil was used to consecrate a person to be King, Priest, and Prophet. Today it is still used in the coronation ceremony of the King or Queen of England, and is used in liturgical churches to ordain its ministers. This meaning of blessed oil as an agent of consecration makes it useful in commissioning a supplicant for some special task as part of spiritual or relational healing. When a relational wound exists between husband and wife or father and child, I might anoint the supplicant as I pray for the Lord to strengthen him to fulfill his family role.

3. Blessed candle

I have a special affection for blessed candles. They were a part of everyday religious life in my family. When a thunder storm was coming, my mother would tell me to light the blessed candle and to say a prayer for protection. Lighting the candle was a great privilege for me. As the sky darkened and lightening flashed and peals of thunder broke upon us, the burning candle made it easier for me to believe that Christ was present and would protect us.

A lighted candle carries more than one symbolic meaning. It reminds us that Jesus is the Light of the world and that he has overcome the darkness. It is also a symbol of welcoming. For a special person or a special occasion, we set the dinner table with lighted candles. During ministry, we light candles in the room to welcome the supplicant as a special person and to remind her that Christ is present. The candles help draw her into the presence of God.

As a team begins to prepare itself for ministry, lighting a candle signals a change. Social conversation is ended. The team is drawn into a conscious recognition of God's presence. A lighted candle transforms an ordinary room into a sacred place. Faith is aroused. We can more easily believe that Jesus is with us in this ministry.

Teams sometimes place a candle in the hands of a supplicant during ministry when things seem especially painful or hopeless for her, or when she is being commissioned to be a light to others as a result of her healing.

Candles, in fact all sacramentals, are especially helpful when ministering to young children. Symbols convey God's presence and care when words won't. You may need to invent sacramentals for them. One team blessed helium-filled balloons. Then they tied symbols of the child's hurts on them and had the child go outdoors and release them to indicate that Jesus would take the hurts away.

4. Blessed salt

As a natural element, salt carries symbolic meanings that are important in the ministry of healing prayer. It is a condiment used to enhance the flavor of food. Jesus had this use of salt in mind when he called his disciples "the salt of the earth" (Mt 5:13). Salt is used as a preservative to keep food from spoiling. Some people use it as an antiseptic to prevent infection of a wound. Mindful of these meanings, Christians use blessed salt to combat Satan and other forces of evil. So when a supplicant is involved in a spiritual or moral struggle, blessed salt is a valuable sacramental. The team might sprinkle the place of ministry with blessed salt during the preparation time. The team or the supplicant could be sprinkled during ministry. I have used it successfully with supplicants who are struggling to break addiction to nicotine. I give the supplicant a small vial of blessed salt and recommend that he place a few grains on his tongue and call upon the Lord to meet his needs when he craves nicotine.

For Further Reading

1. *Redeemed Creation: Sacramentals Today,* by Laurence R.X. Brett. Michael Glazier Co., 1984.

Summary—Chapter 15

A. The prototype for all sacramentals is the Incarnation—Jesus, the Word made flesh. The invisible, intangible reality of God became known to us through the visible human life of Jesus.

   1. Through sacramentals, the fruits of God's creation, ministers of religious healing can help supplicants experience the reality of God's presence more fully.

   2. Sacramentals differ from the sacraments of the church, which ordinarily are administered only by an ordained minister.

B. Four sacramentals are used frequently in religious healing:

   1. *Blessed water ("holy water"):* useful as a symbol of cleansing, especially in cases of healing from sexual abuse. Helpful for the prayer team as a reminder that they have been baptized in Christ and are gathering in his name.

   2. *Blessed oil:* useful as a symbol of healing of wounds, especially physical ones. Helps during a time of consecrating or commissioning a supplicant for some special task as a part of spiritual or relational healing.

   3. *Blessed candle:* Helps symbolize God's presence and protection. Useful as a sign of welcome to the supplicant, or as a sign that transforms an ordinary room into a sacred place.

   4. *Blessed salt:* Helps combat the forces of evil, especially when a supplicant is involved in a spiritual or moral struggle. Useful with supplicants who are trying to break an addiction.

For Your Reflection—Chapter 15

1. Psalm 19:1-4 tells us that all of creation makes known some aspect of God: "The heavens declare the glory of God, the vault of heaven proclaims his handiwork. . . . No utterance at all, no speech, no sound that anyone can hear; yet their voice goes out through all the earth, and their message to the ends of the world."(JB) Reflect on those created things that most speak of God to you. Whatever they are, they are sacramentals for you.

2. How many of the four sacramentals discussed in this chapter have you experienced? Reflect on an occasion where you felt blessed as a recipient of one of the sacramentals. Spend a few minutes in prayer, thanking God for the experience, for coming to you through His creation.

3. Have you ever used one of the above sacramentals in ministry? If so, reflect on the ways in which it enabled the recipient to experience God in a deeper way than might have been possible without the sacramental. Then think of future possibilities where you might use the blessings of creation in leading people into an awareness of God's presence.

16

The Laying On of Hands

❖   ❖   ❖   ❖   ❖

Jesus laid his hands upon the sick and healed them (cf. Mt 8:15; 9:29). And he directed his disciples to do likewise. Behind the ritual of the laying on of hands is the fundamental importance of touch for human beings. A human being simply cannot survive in total isolation from other creatures.

Touch is the most elementary way of being connected to others. Each square inch of skin has millions of receptors that constantly take in messages from the environment. We know, for example, that touch is essential to the process of bonding a mother and her newborn infant. Without this connectedness to another human, the infant will fail to thrive and sometimes even die for no medical reason.

In addition to physiological and psychological effects, the experience of being touched has spiritual effects as well. Jesus must have known this because he used touch in ways other than the ritual of laying on hands. He hugged the little children that were brought to him for a blessing (Mt 19:13-15). He reached out and actually touched a leper; perhaps embraced him (Mt 8:1-4). This act brought a man back into society who had been ostracized from all human connectedness for the duration of his illness.

With Jesus as the model, it is not surprising that many of Christianity's principle religious activities involve touch. In Roman Catholic practice, every one of the seven sacraments involves some form of ritual touching.

In the ministry of religious healing, we may use touch in a ceremonial way by extending our hands and laying them lightly upon the head or shoulders of the supplicant. More often, we hold the supplicant's hand or place an arm around his shoulders while seated close to him. On occasion it may be appropriate to embrace the supplicant, or even to hold him. This might be done, for example, when the supplicant is sobbing in grief or other pain. In praying for a child, we might take him upon our lap.

Cautions in Using Touch

Most people respond favorably to the use of touch in ministry. It is a powerful way of becoming connected, and most supplicants want to feel closely connected to the ministers. But cautions need to be observed:

1. Embracing or holding a supplicant is appropriate for team ministry only, **not** for solo ministry!

2. Before using touch, we must make sure the supplicant is comfortable with it. For a variety of reasons, some people are not comfortable with touch, or even with physical closeness. To some supplicants, sitting too close to them seems like a violation of their "space."

   Sometimes we can tell by a supplicant's body language that she is uncomfortable with closeness or touch. She may move away from us or tense up when we come close. **To be safe, always ask the supplicant if she is comfortable with touch or closeness. Do not assume you know the answer to this question!** Even if the person is a member of a group that customarily hugs, she may simply endure this behavior while feeling uncomfortable with it. In these cases, touch hinders ministry.

   I remember ministering on a team and unthinkingly laying my hand upon the supplicant's shoulder as she was sobbing. She flinched and drew back. I withdrew my hand and later asked her if she was uncomfortable with touch. She said that as a child she had been sexually abused by her father. In such a situation, touch of any kind is inadvisable.

3. Any use of touch in ministry that can carry a sexual meaning—such as hugging a person too closely for too long, touching the upper thigh, kissing on the lips—is entirely inappropriate. Ministry by a team safeguards against these meanings, but may not entirely eliminate them.

4. Hands must be laid on gently and with respect. I have experienced prayer ministers laying their hands upon me so heavily that it was a burden. I did not feel respected; instead, I felt I was an object being dominated by the ministers. Needless to say, it was not a healing experience.

With these cautions in mind, we discover that the appropriate use of touch is a way of communicating. We pick up information from the supplicant by touch. We can tell if she is tense or relaxed. We can tell when changes take place as we minister to her. But we also give information about ourselves to the supplicant by touch. That's why the laying on of hands must never be an expression of power. Instead, it must convey the gentle love of Jesus.

For Further Reading

1. *Caring, Feeling, Touching*, by Sidney B. Simon. Argus Communications, 1976.

Summary—Chapter 16

A. Touch can produce physiological, psychological and spiritual effects. Jesus used touch in his ministry. In the Catholic Church, all seven sacraments involves some ritual form of touch.

B. Appropriate uses of touch in team prayer ministry include:

1. Touching a supplicant in a ceremonial way by extending our hands and laying them lightly upon his head or shoulders.

2. Holding or embracing a supplicant who is experiencing profound grief or pain.

C. Cautions about touch:

1. Embracing or holding a supplicant is appropriate for team ministry only, **not** for solo ministry!

2. Before using touch, we must make sure the supplicant is comfortable with it. **To be safe, always ask the supplicant if she is comfortable with touch or closeness.**

3. Any use of touch in ministry that can carry a sexual meaning is entirely inappropriate.

4. Hands must be laid on *gently* and with respect.

D. The appropriate use of touch is a way of communicating. Ministers pick up information about the supplicant and give information about themselves. Therefore, the laying on of hands always must be an expression of *love*, not power.

For Your Reflection—Chapter 16

1. Think of a time when you were hurting and someone instinctively used touch to comfort or console you. Jot down some words that describe what you experienced from that touch. Was the touch helpful? Why or why not? How would *you* touch someone in a similar situation?

2. In Scripture, lepers were those who suffered from a variety of serious or trivial skin diseases, e.g., eczema, ringworm, Hansen's disease (the classic leprosy). People shunned lepers out of fear of contagion. Touching them was seen as high-risk behavior that transmitted the lepers' uncleanness to the one doing the touching. Read Mk 1:40-42 then, in your mind's eye, imagine how Jesus touched this particular leper. Ask Jesus to show you if there is someone in your life whom He wants you to "touch" (emotionally, physically or spiritually). How does He want you to touch this person? Pray for the gift of courage to reach out to him/her.

17

Resting in the Spirit

❖   ❖   ❖   ❖   ❖

Resting in the Spirit is a valuable means of healing for prayer teams. Sometimes called "slain in the Spirit" or "overcome by the Spirit," it can occur at special moments when a supplicant is so filled with the power of the Spirit that his body and the mind need to "rest" from other activities. A common scenario for resting in the Spirit is that a supplicant is being prayed for and falls over backwards.

A casual observer might think that a "resting" person has fainted and is unconscious. This is not so. She is more acutely conscious than usual. She is absorbed in what God is doing within herself and has no energy for other considerations. Psychology would call this an altered state of consciousness.

Most supplicants who are Resting in the Spirit could pay attention to their surroundings if they cared to. (In rare cases, someone may be out of touch with her surroundings.) Usually, however, consciousness is so completely focused on God's activity within that external distractions such as conversations and activities are filtered out. Some people report they cannot resist or even "come out" of Resting in the Spirit by their own volition. However, I believe that if an emergency arose, usually they could do so.

Ministers of healing sometimes super-spiritualize Resting in the Spirit to the point that they leave no room for a natural dimension in it. Our best understanding is that Resting in the Spirit is a natural spiritual phenomenon used by God at special times for his own special purposes. The causes of it are complex and not fully known, but we do know that almost certainly the causes are a mixture of divine and human.

Sometimes the human element can be a greater part of the cause than at other times. For example, human expectancy plays a heavy role. If people come to a large healing service with the expectation that they will Rest in the Spirit, and are even eager for this spiritual experience, it is more likely to happen. Another example of the human element is "group contagion." If it happens to several people in a group, it often spreads to others.

I view Resting in the Spirit as a valuable healing tool to be used only in private.[1] In private, the supplicant who is Resting in the Spirit is less distracted and less self-conscious; this allows the Spirit to operate in her more fully. I believe that Resting in the Spirit should *not* be used in large public gatherings because some people need personal attention which cannot be given in mass meetings. If this needed personal ministry is not available, Resting in the Spirit can be a destructive, rather than a healing, experience.

Because the causes of Resting in the Spirit are a mixture of the divine and human, ministers and supplicants have some, though not total, control of a situation. The ministers can create an atmosphere which facilitates the work of the Spirit in the supplicant. And usually the supplicant can choose to accept or to resist the experience to some degree.

People report a wide range of sensations associated with Resting in the Spirit. If the supplicant enters into it from a standing position, he will feel as though he is floating to the ground. This is deceptive because, in fact, he is not floating, but falling. The fall could injure him, so it is necessary to have someone standing behind him who is strong enough to catch him and lower him safely to the floor. The person may rest there from several seconds to several hours.

---

1. There are other ministers, whom I respect, who advocate the use of resting in the Spirit at large healing services. See Francis MacNutt's book *Overcome by the Spirit* (Old Tappen, N.J., Chosen Books, 1990) for a different point of view and much practical wisdom.

While "resting," some people enjoy a sense of quiet and peace. Although nothing special seems to be happening, they are content to remain in that state for some time. Some feel happiness, joy, or even mirth. One supplicant reported experiencing the Holy Spirit as water flowing over her entire being, refreshing and cleansing her. A sense of the Divine Presence in the form of brilliant light or colors is common. Others report Jesus' presence, effecting physical, emotional or spiritual healing. Often people cry tears of relief or joy.

Occasionally someone will have a bad experience. She may get in touch with painful memories that have not been healed and will need someone to minister to her while she continues to Rest in the Spirit. Although it is not frequent, a person may discover she is troubled by the influence of evil spirits and will need the ministry of deliverance.

I include Resting in the Spirit in the Institute for Christian Ministries' training program. We provide each student with the opportunity to Rest in the Spirit himself, and to minister it to another. By doing this in the training group under staff supervision, it takes Resting in the Spirit out of the realm of the sensational and gives the students a solid basis for using it as a resource in their ministry. We give our students the following information:

How to Minister Resting in the Spirit in Personal Prayer Ministry

Give advance instructions

1. If this is the first time your team has used Resting in the Spirit with a particular supplicant, a team member should explain to the supplicant what it is, what it feels like, and why you thinks it would be beneficial. Ask the supplicant if he is willing to rest in the Spirit. **Do not proceed with it if the supplicant indicates any unwillingness.**

2. Emphasize a desire for the Lord's healing presence, rather than create a fascination with the experience itself.

3. Inform the supplicant ahead of time that he may or may not experience Resting in the Spirit. If it does not happen, this is not considered a failure.

4. Instruct the supplicant that once he is Resting in the Spirit, he should occasionally and briefly tell the team what he is experiencing so they can decide what direction their continued ministry should take.

Move into Resting in the Spirit

1. In ministering Resting in the Spirit, a supplicant usually starts in a standing position while those ministering to him stand before him, with one or two strong people behind to catch him when he falls. **Ministers should not actually lay their hands on the supplicant; you do not want him to feel he is being pushed over.** Instead, hands are held close to the forehead while the team prays, audibly but quietly, that the person will experience an infilling of the Holy Spirit.

2. Music and song may be used.

3. Enter into prayer, asking God to heal the supplicant. This kind of prayer might last anywhere from two to five minutes. Prayer in one's prayer language is useful *if* the supplicant is comfortable with it.

4. If "resting" does not happen within several minutes, do not persist in prayer. To do so only causes tension for everyone. Sometimes a brief conversation with the supplicant will disclose some obstacle that can be dispelled through conversation. The team can then pray once again for the supplicant, and many times he does then experiencing Resting in the Spirit.

5. It is possible to enter into Resting in the Spirit from a position of sitting on the floor with one's legs extended so that only the upper part of the body falls backward. This is useful when the supplicant is especially heavy, the members are too few in number or too weak to catch the supplicant, or the supplicant fears injuring himself in a fall.

6. I've discovered that it is also possible to start from a prone position, but this seems to work well only when the supplicant has previously experienced some actual falling. Allowing oneself to fall seems to be a symbolic action of letting go of control of one's life and giving it over to God. Once having had the experience of surrendering, it then seems possible to Rest in the Spirit while lying down. If you are praying for a person to "rest" from the prone position, it is necessary to have your hands upon him to detect the perceptible release of muscle tension which is a signal that "resting" has occurred.

During Resting in the Spirit

1. When the supplicant falls back, catch him, gently lower him to the floor and cover him with a blanket. Covering the supplicant makes him feel more secure. Lying on the floor before others causes one to feel vulnerable. Some supplicants worry about an undignified appearance. Being covered reduces these preoccupations.

2. If God's presence is intense and healing, merely pray quietly for the healing to continue. The supplicant's occasional brief reports will guide the team's prayer.

3. If nothing much seems to be happening, quietly proceed according to the plan of action previously decided upon, with the supplicant still "resting." Any one of the four areas—physical, emotional, spiritual, relational—can be ministered to.

4. Do not enter into any long discussion with the supplicant while he is Resting in the Spirit. You may ask him to report what he is experiencing in the way of images, experiences of God, memories, so your ministry will not hinder what the Spirit is doing. Occasionally you might suggest images or report to the supplicant images or thoughts you believe are from the Lord.

The Effects of Resting in the Spirit

Usually long-term prayer ministry with a supplicant includes more than Resting in the Spirit. If a team uses it at all, they combine it with other prayer resources. But sometimes Resting in the Spirit brings healing when nothing else works. I remember being stymied in ministry to woman named Ruth. Whenever one of our team members asked her even a simple clarifying question, she became argumentative, the team got involved in the argument, and all of us became confused. Although we discussed this with Ruth, she seemed unable to control this behavior. So we decided to avoid all discussion and try Resting in the Spirit. Ruth agreed to this and had no difficulty entering into it.

While Resting, Ruth reported being intensely aware of God's presence. Only rarely did we make a suggestion to direct her use of imagery. Mostly we prayed quietly, even silently, sometimes using our prayer language. Occasionally we used recorded instrumental music as we prayed.

Our entire ministry to Ruth consisted of Resting in the Spirit. Each experience lasted about 45 minutes. We told her when the time was drawing to an end gave her time to come out of the "resting" state. Once roused, we gave her time to give added reports of what had happened if she wished, but we did not ask questions and did not discuss her input. We simply spent a short time giving thanks to God for what he had done with Ruth.

After eight sessions of Resting in the Spirit, both Ruth and the team felt she was sufficiently healed to live out her Christian life productively. Now and then, one of the team members had informal contact with her and reported that she continued to show signs of progressive healing over the next several years. Ruth found new joy in life and a new energy that allowed her to undertake a difficult ministry: she opened a shelter for homeless women.

Sometimes one session of Resting in the Spirit can produce a profound breakthrough for a long-term problem. I received the following letter three weeks after a ministry session (reprinted with permission):

Dear Father Leo,

I'd like to share with you my experience of Resting in the Spirit. I remember your praying for me to receive any gift that God had to give. The next thing I was aware of was a beautiful, elderly man. He was ageless: no beginning and no ending. His hair was white and seemed to glow. His eyes were as fire—fire that has burned a very long time. His skin was smooth. Still, he was very old and luminous. His whole being and countenance was love: love so deep that it came from deep burning.

The man looked me directly in the face and said, "Mary, you can trust me." He then took my hand and helped me to my feet. (I was still physically lying down.) After he had helped me to my feet, we were standing side by side. He then began to show me my life: from the moment of conception to now. As my life began to unfold I was standing aside and Jesus was experiencing the things that have happened to me.

I saw him being molested and raped, and I was unwounded. I saw him experiencing the inability to speak, to walk, to communicate, and I was not scared. I saw him frozen in fear and in terror, and I was able to live, to desire life. I saw him become the adult I became—bitter, frightened, full of grief. I saw that I was no longer that way, that I had become a different person than the events of my life had caused me to be.

Later, as I grasped the horror that was happening, I wanted to rescue Jesus. But I just stood there while this beautiful old man held my hand. Throughout this part, it seemed that his strength was pouring into me as he held my hand.

While all this was going on, there was a tremendous noise, like a boom when the sound barrier is broken. Every molecule of my being was changed. Father Leo, this experience has stayed with me. Three weeks have passed since I first began to set this down. Finally it is all down. God bless you.

For Further Reading

1. *The Falling Phenomenon,* by Theodore E. Dobson. Dove Publications, 1986.
2. *Overcome by the Spirit,* by Francis MacNutt. Revell Co., 1990.

Summary—Chapter 17

A. Resting in the Spirit can occur at special moments when someone is so filled with the power of the Holy Spirit that his mind and body need to "rest" from other activities. This chapter asserts that this valuable healing tool should be used only in private healing ministry, rather than in large healing services.

B. How to minister Resting in the Spirit in personal ministry:

1. Give advance instructions; do **not** proceed if the supplicant indicates any unwillingness to participate.

2. Move into Resting in the Spirit:

   a. Usually supplicant starts in a standing position. Ministers should **not** actually lay their hands on the supplicant.

   b. Enter into prayer; music and song may be used.

   c. If "resting" does not happen within several minutes, do not persist in prayer.

3. During Resting in the Spirit:

   a. When the supplicant falls back, catch him, gently lower him to the floor and cover him with a blanket.

   b. If God's presence is intense and healing, merely pray quietly for the healing to continue.

   c. If nothing much seems to be happening, quietly proceed according to the plan of action previously decided upon, with the supplicant still "resting."

     d. Do not enter into long discussions with the supplicant while he is "resting." It is appropriate to ask him to occasionally report what he is experiencing.

For Your Reflection—Chapter 17

1. In a few words, jot down your reaction to this chapter's description of Resting in the Spirit. Would you feel comfortable being the recipient of this type of ministry? Why or why not?

2. Scripture describes a number of instances where people fell prostrate in response to an encounter with God. Reflect on a powerful experience of God that you've had some time in your life. How did you feel physically—weak in the knees? warm and peaceful all over? so relaxed you felt you could stay in that place all day? so aware of God's presence that you only wanted to focus on Him? People who have experienced Resting in the Spirit use these terms to describe the event.

18

Spiritual Gifts

❖   ❖   ❖   ❖   ❖

The stranger phoned me to accuse me of heresy. She had just read an article in which I talked about the Gifts of the Holy Spirit and our need to bring these extraordinary blessings back into the ordinary life of the Church. She disagreed with my article, and called charisms "strange" and people who use them "unstable."

To enlighten the woman, I read her I Cor 12, which describes the early Church's use of charisms such as prophecy and speaking in tongues. She, in turn, stated the classic "dispensationalist" response: "The Church needed dramatic things like that to get itself going; we don't need them anymore." Next I said a Vatican II document urges people to seek God's gifts, even the more extraordinary ones. At this, the woman said, "I don't know if I believe you or not. I need to ask my own priest."

Lay people, theologians and priests alike struggle to understand the mysterious blessings from God that are called Gifts of the Holy Spirit. I count myself among those who struggle. Charisms are so broad and deep that our minds cannot grasp their fullness. But they are vital for the ministry of religious healing. Therefore, I am including this chapter which, first, looks at an overview of God's gifts and, second, describes the spiritual gifts that prayer teams use most often. The goal is to expand learning, remove misunderstandings, and point prayer ministers to local resources.

God's Gifts: An Overview

James told the early Church that "All that is good is given us from above." (NJB, Ja 1:17) In other words, all good within us are gifts from God. I picture these gifts as looking like a three-tier wedding cake. The bottom layer consists of the natural gifts which God gives us at the time of our conception. The middle layer consists of the virtues that we receive at the time of our baptism. And the top layer consists of supernatural gifts of the Holy Spirit. In my view, gifts of the Spirit are natural gifts that are raised to a supernatural level by the power of the Holy Spirit.

Here, then, is how I envision God's gifts:

Gifts of the Holy Spirit
e.g., prophecy, glossolalia,
healing, revelatory gifts

Supernatural Virtues
e.g., prudence, temperance, fortitude,
justice, faith, hope, love

Natural Gifts
e.g., all creation, arts/science technology,
one's individual, genetic gifts

Natural Gifts

Every child enters the world with a variety of gifts already in place. At the time of our conception, God blesses each of us as a unique part of creation: "It was you who created my inmost self, and put me together in my mother's womb; for all these mysteries I thank you: for the wonder of myself, for the wonder of your works." (JB, Ps 139:13-14)

Our natural gifts are a part of God's whole creation and are a blessing to us and to the world. One person may be given a gift of physical coordination; another, a gift of math; still another, a gift of common sense. In fact, God has given each of us many natural gifts. We need to discover them and develop them through study and practice. They form the foundation upon which the supernatural gifts can stand.

Once in awhile someone is born with a dramatic talent. Mozart comes to mind. He probably represents the man in Jesus' parable of the three servants (Mt 25:14-30) who received five talents from his master. Most of us receive less sensational, or less easily recognized, gifts; yet God gives each of us talents—our natural gifts—and asks us to "invest" them in education and practice so that we can use them to bless and serve others.

Natural gifts are essential in healing ministry. In Chapter 2, our prayer team used many of them. Iris' gift of hospitality and her skills in decorating helped us create a warm, safe place for our supplicant. Jim's gift of music helped us enter into wholehearted praise and thanksgiving. My training at the Menninger Foundation gave me an awareness of possible emotional needs that Gloria might have.

The list of natural gifts that are useful in healing ministry is nearly endless. In my experience, God never wastes any of the natural gifts we have developed throughout the course of our lives. In this ministry, every bit of knowledge and skill we possess eventually gets used—often at surprising moments.

Supernatural Virtues

At the time of our baptism, God blesses us with supernatural "virtues," those spiritual gifts we need in order to become the sort of person Jesus was and is. Virtues give us the grace to obey the Ten Commandments, but they also do more than that: they empower us to live as Jesus lived.

Virtues are ways of being in relationship. The God-oriented ones—faith, hope and love—primarily involve our relationship with God. Secondarily, they spill over into our relationships with people. The people-oriented virtues—justice, prudence, courage and temperance—primarily involve our relationships with people. Secondarily, they impact our oneness with God.

Virtues are required for ministry! They give us the ability to live out Jesus' command to "be perfect as your heavenly Father is perfect." (Mt 5:48) Yet some people neglect them. When this happens, the supernatural gifts of the Holy Spirit become sources of harm instead of healing. Charisms can be abused so badly that they eventually harm the ministry, the minister and the supplicants. A few televangelists have destroyed their ministries and reputations because they concentrated on their natural and supernatural gifts while neglecting their virtues.

Scholars spend whole lifetimes studying and writing about God's virtues. Here I offer a brief sketch of them. In reality, all the virtues are inseparable. Hope is faith in action, faith without love is useless, etc. For the sake of discussion, though, each one is described separately.

1. The virtue of faith

This is the God-given ability to radically commit ourselves to being in relationship with Christ. From this flows the power to live in a Christ-like way. But committing ourselves to Christ is not a one-time act. Faith grows (or lessens) as we allow (or disallow) it to govern our entire life—the way we think and act.

This virtue—our commitment to Christ—can come under severe attack. Jesus' disciples experienced a crisis of faith when many followers abandoned Jesus. When he asked them if they also would like to leave, Peter said, "'Lord, to whom would we go? You have the words that give eternal life. And now we believe and know that you are the Holy One who has come from God.'" (TEV, Jn 6:67-69)

The virtue of faith keeps us connected to Christ, who tells us that "you can do nothing without me." (TEV, Jn 15:5b) Without faith, healing ministry could not exist because we could not make God real to our supplicants. Yet the temptation exists to skip over our personal relationship with God and get on with the more exciting aspects of ministry. We need to keep actively seeking growth in our faith life, or we risk becoming mere functionaries—robots for God who go through the paces of ministry but bear little fruit.

2. Love (sometimes called charity)

This is best expressed by the Greek word *agape*. Agape is total dedication to the welfare of others, regardless of personal cost. This type of love is natural only to God, but He gives us a share in it at the time of our baptism. It first unites us to God, and then is directed to other humans. Jesus demonstrated agape toward us, then told us to show it to God and to people: "I give you a new commandment: love one another. As I have loved you, so you must love one another." (TEV, Jn 13:34)

Agape love must be *the* primary motive for all ministry because ministry is service to others, on behalf of the Body of Christ, for the sake of the Reign of God. It is not something we choose to do for humanitarian or self-centered reasons. Rather, we minister to others because God calls us to do so, and we respond to that call out of *loving* obedience.

The ministry of religious healing will cost us a lot: time, money, energy, the pain of sharing in people's suffering. Only love will enable us to pay the price this ministry demands of us.[1]

3. Hope

Hope gives us the ability to believe that there is more to reality than our natural minds can grasp. In the presence of seemingly hopeless situations, hope enables us to see God's infinite love, wisdom and healing power.

Healing ministry must include hope as a major goal, because without this virtue, healing cannot take place.[2] To a greater or lesser degree, all supplicants need us to help them bolster their level of hope. This cannot happen unless we ourselves possess this virtue. To raise a supplicant's level of hope, we must depend on this virtue rather than on our own human resources. With hope, we come to believe that God is caring for our supplicants in ways surpassing our ability to grasp.

---

1. Chapter 4 of *Healing as a Parish Ministry* goes into detail about the price we pay to engage in healing ministry.

2. Chapter 9 of *Healing as a Parish Ministry* is called "The Enemy Within." It goes into depth about hopelessness as a major problem for supplicants. Taken to an extreme, hopelessness can even cause death.

4. Prudence

Prudence does *not* mean caution, timidity or conservatism. Instead, it resembles what we mean when we talk about "common sense." It is the God-given power to decide what is the best thing for *this* person in *this* situation.

Every prayer team needs the virtue of prudence! In ministry we constantly face decisions as to how to proceed with supplicants, because people rarely come to us with one, isolated problem. For instance, in Chapter 3, the St. Mary's prayer team had to continually pray for specific ways to proceed with Larry. The virtue of prudence and the charism of discernment are partners in ministry. No one's discernment is flawless (as the St. Mary's prayer team demonstrated in their early ministry to Larry). Therefore prudence provides a safety-net for the charism of discernment. Discernment without prudence/common sense can go far afield from what God actually wants to do with a supplicant.

5. Justice

Justice concerns itself with the rights of others and with our responsibilities regarding those rights. On the surface, this virtue doesn't seem to involve healing ministry at all. Yet justice is the reason for the existence of Catholic hospitals and Catholic charities. The Church believes that wounded people have a *right* to competent care.

What holds true for medical and charitable care also applies to the ministry of religious healing. The virtue of justice forms the foundation for what we do. The parable of the Good Samaritan is our model. Supplicants in the throes of physical, emotional, spiritual or relational pain need and deserve our help. And that help must be competent because when we minister to someone who is hurting, we are, in fact, ministering to Christ himself. Justice dictates that we maintain confidentiality, that we are knowledgeable about this ministry, that we are continually developing our relationship with God, that we are loyal to our teammates. To do all this requires God's grace, which comes to us in the form of the virtue of justice.

6. Temperance

Popular use of the word temperance during this century has warped our understanding of it as a virtue. Now most people think of it only as regards alcohol. But this virtue empowers us to use wisely our desires for the pleasures of food, drink and sex. Temperance is linked to asceticism, those practices which help us in the on-going struggle between the spirit and the flesh.

The primary use of temperance in healing ministry is to empower prayer ministers to relate to supplicants and to each other in sexually healthy ways. We need to pray for this virtue because the ministry of religious healing tends to leave people's normal emotional barriers to one another. This may allow inappropriate sexual feelings to emerge which, even if not acted upon, distract everyone from focusing on God and on the supplicant's healing.

7. Fortitude

Fortitude is God's gift of courage. It has both an active and passive side. The active side empowers us to take bold action for the sake of the Reign of God. When persecuted, the early Christians prayed, "Lord, allow us, your servants, to speak your message with all boldness. Reach out your hand to heal." (TEV, Acts 4:29-30a) Today, ministers of religious healing need the same prayer and the same boldness.

The passive side of the virtue of fortitude gives us strength to endure pain, suffering and hardship for the sake of the Reign of God. In healing ministry, it expresses itself in our ability to be patient and persevering in overcoming frustration when ministry with a supplicant is not going well or when it is long-lasting. In Chapter 3, the St. Mary's prayer team needed this virtue when they were tempted to quit parish healing ministry entirely, simply because of their sense of failure with Larry.

Gifts of the Spirit

The gifts of the Spirit are not *things*, like wrapped presents from God; instead, they are *ways* of doing an activity, namely serving the People of God lovingly. As stated earlier, the gifts of the Holy Spirit are those *natural* talents and abilities that the Holy Spirit raises to a *supernatural* level.

Say, for instance, God blesses "Maxine" at birth with a gift of verbal expression. With no thought of God, she develops this gift through education and practice, until she becomes an outstanding speaker. Later she moves into a deep, personal relationship with Jesus. She begins to pray before writing her speeches. Before stepping up to a podium, she asks the Spirit to anoint her words. On a number of occasions, the Holy Spirit elevates Maxine's natural gift of speech to a supernatural level. After some speeches, people tell her that her words are "inspired;" they have made a profound impact on their lives.

Maxine gave fine speeches before she gave her life to God. But when the Spirit gave her a gift of anointed speaking, the impact of her words on others moved to a new, supernatural level that was beyond her personal power to achieve. She recognized and accepted her gift as a blessing the Holy Spirit had bestowed on her *for the benefit of the community.* "Each one, as a good manager of God's different gifts, must use for the good of others the special gift he has received from God." (TEV, 1 Pt 4:10)

Misunderstandings About Gifts of the Holy Spirit

The gifts of the Spirit provoke disagreement in today's church for the same reasons they did 2,000 years ago: people either don't understand them, or they misuse them. When St. Paul told the Corinthians he wanted to "clear up a wrong impression about spiritual gifts" (JB, 1 Cor 12:1), he addressed a need that went beyond the community at Corinth. The same issues, questions and problems that troubled people then still exist today.

Today's church contains several renewal groups that have blessed the Body of Christ. One of these is the Charismatic Renewal, which opened the Church to recognize again the gifts of the Spirit that had lain dormant for centuries. Unfortunately, some charismatics divide the Body of Christ into two parts: those who display charisms—the gifts of the Spirit—and those who do not. And some traditional, non-charismatic Christians think that people who display charisms are emotionally unstable.

I disagree with both these positions. This kind of polarization harms our ability to bring God's healing to a wounded world. I believe Christians can come together and serve God if they give up a few myths that people have about the supernatural gifts of the Holy Spirit.

Myth #1: There are only a few gifts of the Spirit. Actually, gifts of the Holy Spirit are mentioned in a number of places in Scripture (e.g. 1 Cor 12-14; 1 Cor 7:7; Rm 12; Eph 4:11; 1 Pt 4:9-11). At the time of his Ascension, Jesus told his apostles, "When the Holy Spirit comes upon you, you will be filled with power, and you will be witnesses for me . . . to the ends of the earth." (TEV, Acts 1:8) He did not itemize the specifics of that power, which came to the apostles at Pentecost in the form of many gifts. That's because any natural gift from God can be raised to a supernatural level by the power of the Spirit.

Myth #2: The gifts of the Spirit are dramatic. Indeed, a few spiritual gifts attract a lot of attention, especially from those who are unfamiliar with them. A man coming to his first prayer meeting and hearing people speak in tongues may be frightened by the apparent drama of what he hears.

Most gifts of the Spirit, however, are widespread and non-flashy. How many people get worked up by a woman's gift of administration or a man's gift of almsgiving? Yet Paul called these gifts, and stressed that all spiritual gifts are meant for service, not for fanfare.[3]

Myth #3: With gifts of the Spirit, whatever happens is only God's doing. This myth usually is expressed when someone is affirmed for a ministry he has just participated in. If, say, he is affirmed for a gift of healing, he may say "Oh, I didn't do anything; it was the Lord." If this were true, then the minister of religious healing need not have shown up for ministry. God could have taken care

---

3. Both Peter and Paul listed different gifts each time they mentioned them in their letters. This indicates that both the apostles intended to give Christians examples of gifts (vs. a definitive list).

of the problem from above, with no human involvement whatsoever.

People who believe this myth can cause a lot of trouble because they feel no responsibility for what God has given them. If it is the Lord alone who, for instance, utters a prophecy, how can the community question what is said? With this myth, there's no room for the gift of discernment of spirits. And then trouble begins!

An incarnational attitude sees every gift as a shared one: the Spirit gives and empowers; we receive what has been given, shape its expression as a unique child of God, and humbly use it; and the community discerns the presence of that gift and encourages us in our use of it.

Myth #4: *The use of charisms is optional for Christians.* Anyone who believes this myth needs to reread the Parable of the Three Servants (Mt 25:14-30 and Lk 19:11-27). Things did not go well for the servant who buried his talents. Jesus used a verbal two-by-four to attract everyone's attention to this myth. His strong use of words in the parable ("You worthless, lazy lout! . . . Throw him into the darkness outside. . . .") made it clear that God wants and expects us to use *all* the gifts we are given—including gifts of the Spirit.

Giving up this myth can pose problems, however. We do not instinctively know what gifts we have been given. It's difficult to use what we do not know we possess. Also, any gift requires practice in order to bloom into its fullest beauty. I suggest the following solutions to these problems.

How to Discover and Develop Gifts of the Spirit

A book can only go so far in helping people learn and grow. Imagine what would have happened if Mozart had only read about music and had never taken lessons or even sat down at a piano. His gift of music would have remained dormant within him, and the world would have been deprived of music that has the power to heal our souls and make our spirits soar.

Ministers of religious healing who want to discover and develop their gifts need to find resources where this can take place. I suggest local charismatic prayer meetings. Most areas have prayer meetings that take place on a regular basis, and these can be a rich resource for teaching, personal discovery and growth. Some prayer meetings offer "Life in the Spirit" seminars. These take place over the course of several sessions and lead up to what commonly is called "Baptism in the Spirit."[4]

People usually use the term "Baptism in the Spirit" to describe that moment when we ask God to send down the Spirit and "release" the supernatural gifts of the Spirit. Some people receive the gift of tongues (glossolalia) at that time; some do not. Almost all of them, however, have a felt experience of God's presence—a feeling of peace, a warm glow, tears of joy, etc. The feelings vary.

Usually we discover one or two spiritual gifts at the time we become baptized in the Spirit. These need to be experienced and put into practice within a loving, supportive community. Also, it is common for other spiritual gifts to be discovered over the days, weeks, months and even years following the initial release of spiritual gifts. In short, a one-time event will not enable spiritual gifts to reach their full potential. Just as humans need three meals a day in order to be healthy and energetic, we ministers of religious healing need regular experiences of prayer, practice and community support for our gifts to blossom.

One caution: Not all prayer groups are equal in wisdom and wholeness. Some can conduct themselves in ways that harm people. In my experience, prayer groups that are accountable to church authorities tend to be more spiritually mature than non-

---

4. In the early Church, "Baptism in the Holy Spirit was synonymous with the rite of Christian Initiation—i.e. Baptism in water, Confirmation and Eucharist. Among other effects, the rite bestowed the charisms/gifts of the Holy Spirit. With the practice of infant Baptism, the powerful spiritual experience of receiving the Holy Spirit was lost.

Today's "Baptism of the Holy Spirit" that takes place in prayer groups refers to communal prayer with an individual for the release of the power of the Holy Spirit and an activation of the graces and gifts already received in the rites of Christian Initiation (Baptism, Confirmation and Eucharist).

affiliated ones. If one group does not seem to fit your style or meet your needs, I suggest trying out another prayer group for awhile. We all need safe, nurturing places within which we can grow. I encourage you to seek out one of those places so you can learn about, discover and use the gifts of the Spirit.[5]

Specific Gifts of the Spirit

Whole books have been written about the various gifts of the Spirit. It would be impossible for me to do justice to any one of them in this short space. Instead, I will briefly describe those gifts of the Spirit that ministers of religious healing use on a frequent basis. Also, I will show how they can be used to help bring about healing through prayer ministry.

1. Praying in tongues (glossolalia)

Of all the gifts of the Spirit that exist, glossolalia has caused more disturbances—literally and figuratively—than any of the others. Paul chided the Corinthians about the manner in which they were using glossolalia in public worship gatherings: "If then, the whole church meets together and everyone starts speaking in strange tongues—and if some ordinary people or unbelievers come in, won't they say that you are all crazy?" (TEV, I Cor 14:23) Those same thoughts persist today. Many non-charismatics think that people who pray in tongues have slipped into a trance or a temporary state of nonsense.

This is not true. Instead, the gift of tongues is language without conceptual meaning. It is a "meta-language," meaning something that goes beyond normal language and the limits of the human intellect. A secular, non-religious meta-language can be heard with jazz singers like Ella Fitzgerald who switch to "scat" singing when the music moves them to a point beyond words.

With glossolalia, the Spirit empowers us to pray beyond words: "The Spirit comes to help us, weak as we are. For we do

---

5. For Catholics, I recommend prayer groups that meet within the support of a Catholic diocese and, preferably, a parish.

not know how we ought to pray; the Spirit himself pleads with God for us in groans that words cannot express." (TEV, Rm 8:26)

The important thing to remember about the gift of tongues is that it is prayer. When we pray in tongues, we communicate with God with the intent of offering praise and thanks or, sometimes, petition. This makes it very useful for prayer ministry, especially at those moments when we do not know exactly how to intercede for a supplicant.

Personally, I find that praying in tongues opens me up to other gifts of the Spirit, especially the gifts of discernment and wisdom. Before beginning to pray in tongues, we may feel completely "stuck" in a ministry session. Glossolalia enables us to focus simultaneously on God and the supplicant in such a way that we begin to sense what we need to do next, or what the basic issue is, or what Scripture passage would be appropriate at this moment for the supplicant.

Also, the gift of tongues is very useful for extended prayer (sometimes called "soaking" prayer). If, for instance, a team spends one hour a week for six weeks praying for healing for a supplicant's torn knee cartilage, it doesn't take too long for everyone to run out of things to say! Praying in tongues can last for many minutes without exhausting people's minds or distracting them from their focus on God and on the supplicant.

One caution: Teams should not use the gift of tongues out loud unless the supplicant is comfortable with its use! Glossolalia can scare people who are unfamiliar with it. It can frighten them away from prayer ministry. However, ministers can pray in tongues under their breath, *provided* they do so without being heard by the supplicant.[6]

2. Gifts of healing

When people think about a healing charism, they often think only about physical healing. Yet supplicants come to us

---

6. Since glossolalia is a non-conceptual language, it's impossible to use it just mentally, inside one's mind. Most people find they must move their tongues in order to exercise this spiritual gift. For this reason, the expression "praying in tongues" seems very appropriate.

with emotional, relational and spiritual wounds, as well as physical ones. (See Chapter 6, "Four Kinds of Wounds.") No single gift of healing deeply touches each of these wounds. So we need to expand our vision to see that God blesses the Body of Christ with many healing gifts.

Ministers who have been given a powerful *gift of physical healing* attract attention if their gift becomes known beyond a small circle. Desperate people flock to them for help. The constant demand for ministry can lead to exhaustion. It also can be spiritually tempting, as Paul and Barnabas discovered after the healing of the man who had been crippled from birth:

> When the crowds saw what Paul had done, they started shouting . . ., "The gods have become like men and have come down to us!" The priest of the god Zeus . . . brought bulls and flowers to the gate, for he and the crowds wanted to offer sacrifice to the apostles. (TEV, Acts 14:11,13)

The apostles' response was to tear their clothes (a gesture of protest), rush into the crowd and shout, "Why are you doing this? We ourselves are only human beings like you! We are here to announce the Good News." (TEV, Acts 14:15a) Those who have a gift of physical healing would do well to remember Paul's and Barnabas' words whenever they feel impressed with themselves as a result of the public acclaim they are likely to encounter.

Gifts of emotional and relational healing, are harder to discern because these types of healing usually are more subtle than physical ones. A man who throws his crutches aside when his shattered knee is healed will cause a sensation. A woman who can sleep again after she is healed of the aftermath of a robbery will not attract attention to herself or to the prayer minister whose gift of emotional healing was used in ministry.

A *gift of spiritual healing* is extremely valuable in the ministry of religious healing, yet it, too, is often undervalued or unrecognized. And as I discussed in Chapter 6, most serious wounds of one type (e.g. physical) impact all other areas of one's being. A supplicant who seeks physical healing for her multiple sclerosis may ask us why God "did this" to her. Even if she becomes healed of her physical illness, she still will need spiritual healing for her misconceptions about God and her anger at him. Every prayer team needs at least one member who has a gift of spiritual healing. (Ideally, every prayer team needs to have each type of healing gift present, but this rarely occurs.)

One final point about gifts of healing: Within a given type of healing, ministers' gifts are diverse. For instance, one minister may be especially gifted in working with children, another with the elderly. In the area of physical healing, Francis MacNutt says he sees remarkable things happen when he prays for people with bone problems, but he says his prayers bear little fruit with people suffering from hearing losses. MacNutt also points out that those who have been healed of a particular problem (e.g. alcoholism) may then receive a special gift of healing for those still afflicted with the same illness.[7]

3. The gift of wisdom

The gift of wisdom empowers us to see a situation through the eyes of God. Our acquired knowledge, life experiences and spiritual maturity lay a strong foundation for this supernatural gift. It is not usually displayed by those who have not yet developed their natural abilities or who do not know much about the truths of faith.

In prayer ministry, the gift of wisdom is a subtle, non-flashy charism. It is the right word, at the right moment, for a particular situation. It helps a supplicant move towards working out a problem, a situation or a relationship. Often it emerges gradually and may be used a number of times during the course of ministry.

I find the gift of wisdom to be invaluable in ministry because supplicants often come to us with overwhelming problems. We need God's vision to know the direction our ministry should take. For instance, in Chapter 3 Larry presented a mountain of needs to the St. Mary's prayer team: unemployment, chronic

---

7. MacNutt, Francis, *The Power to Heal*, Ave Maria Press, Notre Dame, 1977, pp. 95-97.

pain, marital problems, financial disasters and low self-esteem from childhood wounds. Initially the team panicked and ministered poorly. But as they applied their acquired knowledge from earlier training, they opened themselves up to the gift of wisdom. They saw that Larry's damaged self-esteem was the core problem. He confirmed that by choosing to deal first with his childhood wounds. During the ensuing weeks, the team often used the charism of wisdom when deciding what to do next.

4. The gift of knowledge

In healing ministry, the gift of knowledge enables prayer ministers to know something about a supplicant that is not known by natural means. Say, for instance, "Patti" asks a team for prayer because she suffers from anorexia nervosa. She weighs 85 pounds yet says she feels "fat" and can't bring herself to eat. When the team enters into prayer with her, one team member begins to sense that years ago Patti had an abortion, and her anorexia arises from unresolved issues about that event. This information has not been offered by the supplicant—indeed, she is unaware of the connection between the anorexia and the abortion. Instead, this is a "word" of knowledge, i.e., a gift of knowledge for a specific need at a specific moment.

As with other times when we listen to God, the gift of knowledge comes to us in different forms. If we normally sense God in a visual way, we may mentally see a supplicant in a scene from her childhood. If we tend to sense God through hearing, we may hear Him speak something to us. And if we access God through our feelings, we may have a "feeling" about some information. Often a word of knowledge is faint in its intensity and clarity.

All human encounters with God are filtered through the mind, which is influenced by culture, education, religious affiliation and past experiences. So even when we strongly sense a piece of information about a supplicant, we need to remember what Paul told the Corinthians: "Our gifts of knowledge and of inspired messages are only partial; but when what is perfect comes, then what is partial will disappear. What we see now is like a dim image in a mirror." (TEV, 1 Cor 13:9,12a)

The gift of knowledge in the hands of an immature or misguided prayer minister can be disastrous! Imagine the outcome in Patti's situation if the one who senses knowledge about her past blurts out, "God just told me that you had an abortion a long time ago." If the information is correct, she probably will feel stripped of her privacy and dignity, concluding that the team can read her mind and see every past sin. This almost certainly will drive her away from all prayer teams and, therefore, from healing. On the other hand, if the information is incorrect, she will feel wrongly accused and might spread a message to others that prayer ministers are "nuts."

To prevent disasters like this, I offer three suggestions:

- With any word of knowledge, pray for the gift of discernment as to how to use it. Not all messages from God are meant to be shared with a supplicant. Often God gives information to ministers to show them the root cause of a problem and to help them determine a plan for ministry. If a word of knowledge has the potential for being distressing to a supplicant (such as wounds from childhood abuse), ministers should *not* reveal that until they have prayed about it without the supplicant being present (ideally, during debriefing after ministry and during preparation for ministry the next time).

- When sharing a word of knowledge with a supplicant or even with team members, do not name God as its source. It is the Christian community's responsibility (including the supplicant's) to discern the source of a word of knowledge. A word may come from God, or it may simply express the wishes or the biases of the minister. Occasionally, it may even be a lie that comes from Satan.

- When revealing a word of knowledge to a supplicant, I usually use a tentative approach. In Patti's case, after trust has been built up over several sessions of ministry, and after discernment prayer during debriefings as to her readiness, someone might share a vision with Patti that she is receiving, e.g., "I have this mental picture of you. You look like you're in your late teens, and you're crying about something that's just happened. Does that mean anything to you?" Often the supplicant will say "no." She may not have made the connection between the event and your question, she may not be ready to remember the event, she may not be ready to allow you into this part of her past, or you may be mistaken. In any case, you have done no harm, and you've given her an opportunity to reflect on your question between ministry sessions. Supplicants frequently return to our questions long after we've asked them.

5. Discernment of spirits

In prayer ministry, it is vital that we be able to discern the sources of the thoughts, actions and feelings that ministers and supplicants experience. What I said about a particular "word" of knowledge holds true for other thoughts and feelings in ministry: An experience that is proposed as coming from God may come from that source, or it may arise from a purely human source, or it even may be the work of evil spirits.

For example, in Chapter 7 I described my friend Father Anthony, who died of cancer at the age of 40. When he received his diagnosis, everyone prayed fervently for him, and several people prophesied that he would be healed. When Father Anthony got worse instead of better, these prophecies caused confusion and pain for everyone, especially for him. He wrestled with feelings of guilt (about his possibly blocking the healing that God wanted), anger (at God and himself) and depression (at the downhill course of his illness). He might have gone through all these feelings anyway, but the false prophesies intensified them.

When our prayer group reflected on Father Anthony's continued illness, we saw that what had appeared to be a word from the Lord was, in fact, our human longing for a loved one to be healed. In the absence of the gift of discernment of spirits, we had pursued a path of ministry that had not helped our supplicant.

Every team needs this spiritual gift, especially during the assessment phase of the cycle of ministry (Chapter 3). When combined with the gift of wisdom and the virtue of prudence, discernment of spirits can help us devise a plan of action for our ministry that will lead a supplicant towards healing.

6. Inspired use of Scripture

The gift of inspired use of Scripture guides us to select a passage from Scripture that speaks as a living word to this supplicant at this particular time. This gift helps make God personal and real to a supplicant through well-chosen words in Scripture. What has previously been a musty, flat, 2,000-year-old text suddenly comes to life for the supplicant. God speaks personally to him!

The fruits of this spiritual gift can be powerful. For instance, in 1948 I suffered from post-traumatic stress disorder as a result of my experiences in World War II. At a pre-seminary retreat in the midst of that struggle, the retreat-master asked everyone to meditate on Mark 10:46-52—Jesus' healing of the blind beggar. As I entered into the passage, its words seemed to be addressed just to me. Like Bartimaeus, I could feel myself calling, "Jesus! Son of David! Have mercy on me!" And then I sensed Jesus asking me, "What do you want me to do for you?" My answer was the same as Bartimaeus': "Teacher, I want to see again." I wanted and received in 1948 what I still want and receive—a profound, ever-deepening vision of the truth. Whenever I'm struggling with something, I use Mark 10:51 ("Teacher, I want to see again") as a Jesus prayer.

The inspired use of Scripture can give comfort to a supplicant, or confront and challenge her, or give discernment about some issue she is wrestling with at the moment, or bring clarity and understanding about a plan of action. My retreat master obviously felt inspired to ask everyone to meditate on this Scripture passage. It comforted me and helped me discern that God was calling me to become a priest. Its effect on me has persisted throughout my adult life.

Prayer teams that have one or more members with the gift of inspired use of Scripture generally do powerful ministry. As with any other gift, however, this spiritual gift needs to be combined with the gift of discernment of spirits.

Conclusion

Paul told the early Church that all good is a gift from God: "Didn't God give you everything you have?" (TEV, 1 Cor 4:7) Ministers of religious healing who respect, discover, develop and use *all* the gifts God has given them will have a powerful, mature healing ministry. In response to St. Paul's exhortation that we "use our different gifts in accordance with the grace that God has given us" (Rm 12:6a), let each of us pray, "Lord, I accept your gifts. Give me the courage and grace to use them for your glory."

For Further Reading

1. *The Healing Gifts of the Spirit,* by Agnes Sanford. Lippincott Co., 1966.
2. *Catholicism,* by Richard P. McBrien. Winston Press, 1981. pages 965-91.

Summary—Chapter 18

This chapter offers an overview of God's gifts and describes the three levels of gifts that God gives us. All three levels need to be discovered and developed through study and practice.

A. *Natural gifts*: the foundation upon which the supernatural gifts can stand. They are a part of God's whole creation that are intended to be a blessing to us and to the world. e.g., music, medical knowledge, physical coordination, common sense.

B. *Supernatural virtues:* the spiritual gifts we need in order to become the sort of person Jesus was and is. They are ways of being in relationship.

   1. God-oriented virtues primarily involve our relationship with God: *Faith* (the God-given ability to radically commit ourselves to being in relationship with Christ); *love* (total dedication to the welfare of others—first unites us to God, then is directed to other humans); *hope* (the ability to believe that there is more to reality than our minds can grasp).

   2. People-oriented virtues primarily involve our relationships with people: *Prudence* (the God-given power to decide what is the best thing for a given person in a given situation); *justice* (concerns itself with the rights of others and with our responsibilities regarding those rights); *temperance* (empowers us to use wisely our desires for the pleasures of food, drink and sex); *fortitude* (God's gift of courage—both active and passive).

C. *Gifts of the Spirit (charisms):* natural talents and abilities that the Holy Spirit raises to a supernatural level; they are ways of serving the People of God lovingly. Specific charisms include:

   1. *Praying in Tongues (glossolalia):* Language without conceptual meaning. With glossolalia, the Spirit empowers us to pray beyond the limits of our human intellect.

   2. *Gifts of healing:* the ability to be a channel for God to heal someone's physical, emotional, spiritual or relational wounds. Many different healing gifts exist within the Body of Christ.

   3. *Gift of wisdom:* the ability to see a situation through the eyes of God. Acquired knowledge, life experiences and spiritual maturity are a necessary foundation for this charism.

4. *Gift of knowledge:* the ability to know a particular fact that is not known by natural means. Needs to be combined with the gift of discernment in order to be used wisely.

5. *Discernment of spirits:* the ability to know the source of a given thought, action or feeling. The source may be God, human or Satan. An especially valuable gift when combined with the charism of wisdom and the virtue of prudence.

6. *Inspired use of Scripture:* the ability to select a passage from Scripture that speaks as a living word to a particular person at a particular time. Helps make God personal and real to the person.

For Your Reflection—Chapter 18

1. Reflect on what natural gifts God has given you. How many of these gifts are you presently using to bless others? In prayer, thank God for giving you natural gifts, then ask him to show you the ways in which He wants you to use these gifts. What thoughts come to your mind when you ask God this question? Are you willing to say "yes" to using your natural gifts? If you feel hesitant, ask God for the gift of courage.

2. Review the virtues described in this chapter, then think of an event in your life for *each* of these virtues—e.g., an occasion when God gave you prudence, etc. After this, spend a few minutes in prayer, thanking God for these moments of grace. If there are any virtues in which you feel some lack, ask God to bless you with an increase in them.

3. How many of the charisms described in this chapter make you feel uncomfortable? How many have you personally experienced? If you have never been "baptized in the Spirit" (i.e., experienced the power of the Holy Spirit and the release of charisms), are you open to this grace? If your answer is "yes," spend some time looking for options that exist within your geographic area. Ask God to guide you in this process.

4. To grow in awareness of giftedness, choose a few of the Scripture references listed in this chapter and reflect on them: e.g., Jas 1:17a; Ps 139:13-14; Mt 25:14-30; Jn 15:5b; 1 Cor 12-14.

Appendix

Checklist for Self-Evaluation of Prayer Team Ministry

❖　　❖　　❖　　❖　　❖

1. Physical Setting

1. Decorations and arrangement to create the sense of a holy place.
2. Creation of a spiritually warm, inviting spaceby the team.

2. Preparation Phase

1. Leader checks the readiness of the team members to minister.
2. Team members set aside any concerns by giving them to the Lord in prayer.
3. Leader helps the team form a bond of unity and mutual love.
4. Team focuses on preparation for ministry, leaving other kinds of sharing for other times.
5. A brief review of the previous prayer time and plan for this session.
6. Enough prayer time to get the team "in tune" with the Lord and each other.
7. Team members cooperate in preparing for ministry.

3. Ministry

1. The supplicant feels cared for, welcomed.

2. Team works out a plan of action with the supplicant.

3. Supplicant feels listened to, that his/her needs are being taken seriously.

4. Supplicant "receives" the ministry.

5. Leader sets the tone, encourages others to see their gifts, sees that all members are involved.

6. Leader keeps track of the process and helps the team to do so.

7. Team is sensitive to the supplicant and responsive to his/her needs.

8. Team is sensitive to the way the Holy Spirit is moving this session.

9. Team members support the leader.

10. All team members have a role in ministry.

11. Team members respect each other's gifts and roles in ministry.

12. Good closure with the supplicant—stopping at the right point, getting feedback from the supplicant.

13. Supplicant feels better following the ministry; was brought into the presence of Jesus.

14. Supplicant was given clear instructions about future meetings.

4. Debriefing Phase

1. Team reviews the *process* of ministry, rather than only the content.

2. Team reviews how they functioned *as a team.*

3. Team considers what parts of the ministry were and were not effective.

4. Team reassesses the needs of the supplicant.

5. Plan is made for the next session.

6. Leader encourages each team member to reflect on his or her own gifts and *affirms* their use and development.

7. Leader helps team members to express their feelings—positive and negative—about this ministry.

8. Leader encourages the team members to continue the process of discerning their level of ministry.

9. Team leader sees whether prayer was needed by team members as a result of the ministry.

10. Leader "wraps up" the debriefing, perhaps with a prayer for the team as a whole.